JONATHAN AND DAVID BENNETT

The Popular Man Presents:

Be Popular Now

How Any Man Can Become Confident, Attractive and Successful (And Have Fun Doing It)

Jonathan Bennett and David Bennett

Internal Photos and Layout: David Bennett, except below

Photos on pp. 199-201: Joshua Wagner (theconflictmechanic.com)

Cover design: Meg Syverud (megsyv.com)

The Popular Man logo: Natalie Howard (nhoward.com)

Body language modeling (Chap. 33): Natalie Howard

Theta Hill Press

Lancaster, Ohio

thetahillpress.com

Medical Disclaimer

Information in this book is intended as an educational aid only. No information contained in this book should be construed as medical or psychological advice, diagnosis, or treatment. Readers should consult appropriate health professionals on any matter relating to their health and well-being, and before starting any health improvement program.

Copyright © 2013 Theta Hill Press

ISBN: 0615753841

ISBN-13: 978-0615753843

ACKNOWLEDGMENTS

SHOUT OUTS AND THANKS

Jonathan

I'd like to give a special shout out to my family: Carmela, Brianna, and Grace. I'm grateful for their patience and support. I'd also like thank my grandparents and parents, who taught me how to be popular while still having values. My dad deserves special mention since he taught me how to be a popular man who blesses other.

Joshua Wagner deserves a special mention since he taught me a lot about humor, routines, and many other things. He was a great "model" from whom I learned a ton.

I also have to express my thanks to Dave Adams who always reminds me to stay on the right path, especially when stress comes.

I want to offer thanks to the many parents, students, and colleagues who supported me during my teaching days. I'll be forever grateful for the love and kindness I received from all of you.

David

I want to thank my wife Jennifer and daughter Elizabeth. They have put up with my disappearing to coffee shops to work on this project. My parents and grandparents deserve a mention, for raising me to be the stable, fun, popular, handsome (and modest) guy I am!

Joshua Wagner has been a great asset in formulating ideas for this book and for succeeding at life in general. The many hours Jonathan, he, and I spent coming up with various models of success helped make this project possible. Visit him at theconflictmechanic.com. Invite him to speak to your business or organization. You will be glad you did.

I'd also like to thank David Adams, whose rediscovery of the joys of living coincided with my own.

Also, there are many other relatives, students, colleagues, teachers, and friends that have made me what I am today. I have tried to model the best traits from a lot of people, and I am grateful for you all!!

David and Jonathan

Many thanks to Justyn Greene and Andrew Chwalik. Also thanks to Meg Syverud (megsyv.com) and Natalie Howard (nhoward.com) for their graphic design work on this book and various projects, and also to Natalie for modeling for the body language photos in Chapter 33.

CONTENTS

YES, YOU CAN BE POPULAR!

Can you imagine going to a busy club, festival, or business convention and being the center of attention? Everyone there seems to want you. In fact, men and woman come over in big groups and introduce themselves, even barging in on the conversation, just to be a part of the experience of *you*.

Can you imagine walking into a coffee shop and having all the employees gather around you and talk to you, even though other customers are waiting? Oh, and at the end of it all, you get free or discounted food, even as the people in line behind you pay.

Can you imagine having a great social life? Every night you want to go out, you have three or four friends who are practically begging to be at your side. And, that beautiful girl at work you've had your eye on can't stop dropping hints about how much she wants to go on a date.

Can you imagine getting promotions, having unlimited financial opportunities, and becoming more successful and well-connected simply because people like you and find you exciting?

Can you imagine being popular wherever you are?

If you can't really imagine these scenarios, don't worry. You're not alone for thinking popularity is a pipe dream. After all, you'll never be George Clooney, Kim Kardashian, or Justin Bieber. You live five hundred miles from Hollywood. Oh, and you can't act, throw a football, or sing to save your life.

Guess what? None of that matters! You don't need to live in Hollywood or be an actor, athlete, or musician to be a celebrity. You can be popular, and yes, even a celebrity, in any environment, whether it's a small town in Iowa, the college where you study, or your currently boring job.

You see, most people think celebrity equals world famous. While the odds of you achieving that are pretty slim, don't forget that there are countless people who receive the benefits of celebrity status on a local level all the time. They have fame, popularity, money, and the joy of waking up each day knowing that wherever they go, they have fun, get lots of attention, and even bless others.

I know, because I've walked this path. When I was young, I was popular and knew that I was destined for greatness. Other people constantly praised my wit, extroversion, and potential. But, after high school and college, I fell into the rut of being "normal." I settled down, took life way too seriously, and gave up my freedom for an ungrateful employer. I had turned into a boring, typical man that no one paid attention to! My edge was gone. I'd lost the joy that came from being loved and popular.

When I was 31, I lost a job and fell into depression. After a few weeks of pouting, I finally woke up and realized that my life needed a radical change. I didn't want to be average any longer. I wanted to be a confident, happy, and exciting person, the guy I was back in my youth, when the world was mine for the taking. Through my research and practice of successful techniques, and my friendship with excellent people, I left my old patterns behind and became a totally new person. I now live an exciting, fun, and above all, fulfilled life because I am popular and loved everywhere I go.

This book is designed to teach you how to be popular like me. It doesn't matter what environment you happen to be in. That's right: you can achieve popularity anywhere you go and with anyone you encounter. And, my tips have an added advantage. They will help you achieve greater success and increase your contacts so that you can even move beyond your current environment and on to bigger and better things!

Since your experience of so-called popular people, especially in your junior and high school past, may not be the most positive, I want to say a few words about the kind of popularity this book teaches. I will help you make friends, get dates, and attract people of all types into your social circle. You will learn to make yourself more excellent and in the process cut through the drama, stand up to bullies, and enrich the lives of others. I will make you wildly popular while still being positive and inclusive, and living according to your chosen values.

Think again about those scenarios I listed at the start of this introduction. They're not hypothetical. They all describe real events that have happened in my life. And, I have similar experiences every single day. I'm not in the movies, a musician, or a sports star. I'm just a transformed man who is the center of attention wherever he goes. And, it's because I have the techniques to put myself there.

Those skills have also given me the many benefits of being popular: tons of friends, social success with both men and women, amazing networking opportunities, and yes, lots of free stuff. You can have all this too!

I encourage you to read this book slowly. Don't rush just to finish it. Really focus on each chapter and take what I say to heart. What I present is actually very unique and even based on cutting edge brain science. Practice the techniques I give you and follow the suggested activities at the end of each chapter. Yes, you have some homework. But, it's not the pointless stuff you were assigned to keep busy in high school. Practice makes perfect and those activities will help you be popular and beloved as quickly and efficiently as possible.

At The Popular Man have a special offer for you. If you sign up for our mailing list, you can download a free companion workbook. Go to thepopularman.com/bepopularnow to sign up. This workbook will help you complete the practice activities and help you improve your skills more quickly.

CHAPTER 1

A CELEBRITY IS MADE, NOT BORN

Let me tell you a story about a guy you may know. He had big ears and was constantly bullied because of them when he was younger. He was skinny and lanky and even spoke with a bad lisp. He had severe ADHD. In fact, his teacher told his mom "he's not gifted; he'll never be able to focus on anything." Based on this description, I'm pretty sure none of us wants to be this guy! Then again, maybe we do. This awkward, bullied kid grew up into the athletic, good looking, and extremely famous Olympic swimmer Michael Phelps.

Phelps was traumatized by his bullying and self-conscious about his looks. But, he didn't let any of it get him down. In fact, he let his problems motivate him to become an even more excellent swimmer. He "took it out" in the pool. His trainer called Phelps a "motivation machine" where "bad moods, good moods; he channels everything for gain" (1). This story illustrates a crucial truth about not only celebrities, but every popular and successful person in life: you become who you are, not through your situation at birth, but through your effort and your choices.

I'm not going to get into the nature vs. nurture debate here. Certainly your genetics can hinder or help your goals. However, the story of Michael Phelps shows that, with enough passion and effort, even the most awkward among us can achieve their dreams and become successful. In fact, I could share hundreds, if not thousands, of similar stories where some person, no matter his or her disability or disadvantages, beat the odds through working both hard and smart.

Someone who may not have the most advantages in life may even be better off in the long run. What if Michael Phelps had smaller ears or was better at paying attention in math class? Would he have had the same motivation and drive to succeed as an Olympic swimmer? While I can't say for sure, his interviews and the quotes from his trainer seem to indicate he wouldn't be such a successful person today without his adversity.

If you want to become popular, then you have to remember the lesson of Michael Phelps: hard work and practice are the two keys to being successful. Some people may be naturally more outgoing or have less anxiety in social situations. But, it doesn't matter because ultimately being popular requires action. That's right, action. An outgoing, handsome guy who sits at home playing World of Warcraft all day will never become popular. On the other hand, a shy, reserved person who vows to be popular and follows this commitment with learning, practice, and perseverance will end up finding popularity in the end.

A celebrity is made, not born. Repeat that out loud right now. Justin Bieber didn't just come right out of his mom with the perfect haircut and a smooth voice (sorry for the horrific mental image). He worked hard and even went out on the street and sang for the public to have a chance at getting noticed. How many people are willing to endure the possible embarrassment of being a street performer for a chance at success? Not many!

By reading this book, you've made an important first step. You're recognizing, even if subconsciously, that luck, fate, genetics or whatever else, have no bearing on your popularity or lack of it. You have realized that the power to become popular lies only within yourself. The sky is the limit for you. Feeling good about yourself? You should be!

Now I need to give you the bad news. Reading a book about popularity won't make you popular either. It's going to require practice. Don't worry; this kind of practice will be fun and very rewarding. I've also mentioned the phrase "hard work" a lot already, which should clue you in that becoming popular may require some emotionally and mentally difficult tasks. However, don't be scared away. You aren't giving your time to an ungrateful boss or demanding mother. You are working for yourself with an exciting goal in mind: being popular. The best things in life always take some work and this is no different.

Your practice assignment for this chapter seems deceptively easy. You have to believe that even *you* can be popular. Get over your old hang-ups and issues and start to believe in yourself. That's right, starting today you, yes, even *you,* are on the path to popularity. Think about that for a little while.

CHAPTER 2

REALITY: YOU CREATE IT

I'll never forget a story I heard about Marie Antoinette traveling through the Alps on her way to France. While passing through what had to be breathtakingly beautiful scenery, she insisted that the curtains of her carriage be closed. While I can't get into the mind of the unfortunate queen, it seems she preferred the closed world of the tiny carriage to the limitless, abundant beauty of the open wilderness.

Every day, we as humans make a bunch of small choices that tell us a lot about a big thing: our perspective. Perspective, or mentality, is our way of looking at the world. Using perspective, our brains make sense of everything around us. Marie Antoinette's brain must've told her traveling was a burden, the outside world was boring, or both, so she closed the curtains. On the other hand, the brain of a curious, fun loving person would see a trip through the Alps as a beautiful and exciting experience.

The good news is that a person's mentality or perspective doesn't have to be set in stone. Through effort, anyone can change how he views the world. After all, I don't know a person yet who was born an angry, uptight old fogey. By the way, I am getting to the part about popularity soon, so bear with me. This really is important.

The first step to change your perspective on life is to decide what mentality you want. Yes, it's that simple. It could be anything from an open, upbeat mentality to a passionate, driven approach (and everything in between). Then, you make your everyday choices based on your desired mentality. The second step is extremely important. For example, saying "I want to have a happy, relaxed mentality," but freaking out every time life throws you a curve is pretty much pointless.

Most of our lives are lived automatically, so to change our mentality we must turn off auto-pilot and steer a new course. Let's use the example of taking a relaxed mentality. If your roommate is driving you nuts, your automatic response may be to yell at him and storm off, especially if you've reacted that way a thousand times before. But, to be successful at your new goal, you'll have to turn off auto-pilot and take charge of your brain. Your newly chosen perspective now mandates that you tell your roommate calmly and firmly that he is bothering you and he needs to stop.

What all this means is that you create your own reality. If you think life is wonderful and the world is beautiful, then guess what? It will be! On the other hand, if you think life sucks and the world is ugly, then even the most beautiful thing like a trip through the Alps will be terrible. Why? Because everything is mentality and perspective. Everything. Your brain, not your eyes, determines how you see the world.

Let me give you an example of different perspectives. One time when I was in line at Tim Hortons for coffee, a woman butted in front of me and demanded that the cashier fix her order. The employees had given her ham instead of sausage, so she wanted both a refund and a new sandwich. While I don't fault her for wanting the right order, I'm sure a hungry child from Africa would have a totally different perspective on that sandwich, even if it was the "wrong" one.

If you are reading this book, you're probably not in what I call the "popular mentality" yet. Perhaps you're shy, a poor communicator, or hopelessly uptight. Whatever your traits, this book can help you. I was naturally extroverted as a child and teen, but, as an adult, developed all sorts of hang-ups that stopped me from being fun and popular. However, applying the techniques in this book transformed me into a guy people want to be around, a guy whose visit men and women look forward to, a guy who gets perks and benefits everywhere. And, I get it all just for being me!

The best way to get into the "popular mentality" is to follow the advice in this book and do it every single day. Think again about those little decisions you make each day. Well, from now on you will be making yours from the perspective of a celebrity. Everywhere you go and with every choice you make, ask yourself how a celebrity would act and then do that! I know it's easier said (or read) than done. If you're not popular, then it may be hard to convince yourself to act like you are. One way to cut through this mental barrier is to use your mind to your advantage through affirmations, or formally stating what you hope to become.

I recommend that you write a series of these affirmations, or formal statements. Compose them in the present tense, but use the language of process. Use something like "I am becoming popular, attractive, famous, and loved." It's better to affirm that you are becoming, manifesting, materializing, etc. your goals because if you say "I am a popular, attractive, famous, and loved" – and you're not – your brain is likely to counter with "yeah right." However, as you practice the book's techniques and actually become popular, you can alter your affirmations at any time.

You should also follow your affirmations with declarations. These are sentences that declare what you are going to do. Rather than saying what you are hoping to become, these are statements of intent, promises to yourself that you are going to achieve the goals you outline. Use the language of commitment for your declarations. Say something like "I commit to being famous" or "I commit to take on leadership positions at work."

You can then say your affirmations and declarations throughout the day. One little trick I've found is to record a few short affirmations and declarations and then play them back when you get quiet time. Use the "you" form of your affirmations in this case. Say, "You are a famous celebrity" or "Today you are becoming more popular" and so on. After you hear them, repeat them using the "I" form.

By affirming and declaring what you want to achieve, and repeating them on a daily basis, your perspective and the choices you make will begin to change as well. The key is to truly believe your affirmations and follow through with your declarations. The more you say them, the more likely this will occur.

Your mindset determines where you will go in life.

Right now, you may not actually even believe what you're saying. It may be difficult for you to think of yourself as a popular, fun, and happy person beloved by countless people. This doubt is perfectly normal. However, by regularly affirming and declaring your goals, you are essentially convincing yourself of their truth. Affirmations and declarations function as mental cheerleaders inside of your brain. Since your brain likely is filled with unhelpful chatter, they counteract your negative thoughts to help you truly grow into the person you want to become.

Your assignment for this chapter is to write around five to ten affirmations and declarations and say them daily. If you feel up to recording them, I would advise that too. Audacity is good (and free) recording software. Affirmations and declarations are an extremely important subject, but going on about them in detail is beyond the scope of this book. I highly recommend <u>Say It Like You Mean It: How to Use Affirmations and Declarations to Create the Life You Want</u>. The authors of this book are contributors. It gives the topic the attention and space it deserves.

Here are some sample affirmations and declarations, but you should compose your own based on your specific situations. As you read this book, you will want to modify your affirmations and declarations to include what you learn in future chapters.

<u>Affirmations</u>

I am attracting more adoring fans than I know what to do with

I am becoming more outgoing and exciting every day

I am making new friends every day

I am becoming relaxed, cool, and detached

I am receiving the benefits of popularity each day

<u>Declarations</u>

I commit to be outgoing and funny each day

I commit to wake up in a great mood

I commit to make at least five new friends every day

I commit to be wealthy and generous

CHAPTER 3

CHANGE YOUR BRAIN

As I was walking through an upscale mall recently, smiling and confidently approaching people to interact with them, I was struck by how different my life had become. Four years earlier, I had walked through that same mall, but with my head down, too shy to make eye contact with strangers. In addition, I was semi-depressed from a lousy job and on medication to combat anxiety. I sat down with a cup of coffee at Starbucks and just thought for a few minutes about how amazing my personal transformation had been. I was a completely different person. My body language had changed radically, I'd gotten off my meds, and my mentality had completely shifted. I literally saw the world in a different way.

In spite of the last chapter's talk of affirmation and change, from where you're sitting right now, such a change may still seem impossible. This is especially true if you are in a particularly deep rut. However, don't be discouraged. Keep reading. I know from personal experience that change is possible! And, the joy that comes from personal change is unlike anything you've probably ever experienced.

Scientists have long known that the brains of children are highly "neuroplastic," meaning that their brains can rewire as circumstances change. This explains why children can become fluent in a language quickly while you have three years of college Spanish and can barely say "hola." Neuroplasticity is a mechanism that allows humans and animals to grow and develop into functioning adults with ease.

Psychologists used to think that adult brains lacked neuroplasticity. In other words, they believed that your personality and thought patterns were set in stone by the time you reached twenty-five years old. Now that's a depressing thought for all people over twenty-five who aren't where they want to be in life! Of course, that's pretty much everybody in that age bracket. Thankfully, recent research has demonstrated that the adult brain has a good degree of neuroplasticity as well (2). This is an incredible discovery. It means that you can change your brain wiring at any age and watch decades old patterns and habits go by the wayside. Granted, the adult brain isn't nearly as neuroplastic as that of children, but rewiring, with mental intention and focus, is still very possible.

If you think back to your childhood, you can see how unhelpful patterns, through repetition, wired your brain in the first place. Your mother may have been overbearing so now you have trouble relating to women. Maybe you constantly heard from your first grade teacher that you were in the "dumb" reading groups, so you never aimed high. Perhaps your dad always criticized your lack of toughness, so now you suffer from low self-esteem. These beliefs are now literally (and physically) embedded in your mind through brain wiring.

If unhelpful patterns and habits wired your brain in the first place, it follows that the best way to rewire the brain to be popular is to create new patterns and habits by acting and thinking like a celebrity. It will probably require more practice and repetition than when you were a child, because the brain isn't as naturally flexible now. This is why it's vital to say your affirmations and declarations frequently, and to act like a celebrity at all times. This repetition serves to constantly tell your brain that you *are* actually popular. Over time, you will genuinely feel and act like a celebrity naturally because you will have convinced your brain that you are one! It sounds kind of magical, but it works.

Another important point to remember as you rewire your brain through the techniques in this book is that old brain wiring dies hard. Depending on your age, you may have years and years of unhelpful wiring that is hindering you in the present. Even the most dedicated and proficient person training to be popular cannot jettison decades of old wiring in a few days (or even weeks). That means it could take a little while to start developing some confidence. However, it will come. Patience is an undervalued virtue these days, but it's very important to change any aspect of your life.

The best way to fight this old wiring is to use a method called re-framing. A "frame" is a way of seeing and experiencing the world. It is another word for a mentality. Re-framing is changing your way of looking at something, to get a new and more helpful mentality about it (see Chapter 2 for review). For example, most people complain when they get rained on. However, whenever David notices someone complaining about the rain, he humorously points out that people actually pay good money to get wet at water parks. Why don't we enjoy the chance nature gives us to get wet for free? Can you see how this is a re-frame? It is changing one's mentality about a situation (in this case, getting wet) from a negative outlook to a more positive one.

If you find your old ways of thinking re-emerging, and they will, all the time, then you will need to mentally re-frame the situation. Take my day at the mall. I have great new memories there, but also some powerful, and unhelpful, old ones. Let's say I approach a pretty girl and she rejects me. My new brain wiring says, "Who cares?" However, my old brain would want to pout and elicit pity. If those old patterns start to emerge, I must immediately re-frame the situation in light of my new mentality. Rather than let my old frame dominate, I would instead view the situation from my new perspective of detachment (see Chapter 15). Getting rejected by one girl doesn't matter. In addition, I'd find a way to examine the encounter in terms of feedback, rather than failure (Chapter 11). Maybe I bothered her while she was concentrating on shopping and, in the future, I should wait until I receive more signs of openness (Chapter 33).

See how that was done? I used various tools that I've learned over the years to conquer my unhelpful patterns. Of course, having the tools is the first step. Using them is the second. Fortunately, I'm sharing with you the majority of my most helpful tools throughout this book. With time, you will change your brain so much that you will quite literally have a different brain at your disposal, one trained and wired to make you popular and happy.

For this chapter, your assignment is to continue saying your affirmations and declarations and applying what you've learned so far in the real world. Changing your thoughts and your actions are the best way to rewire the brain and become the popular person you know is hiding deep inside of you.

CHAPTER 4

SOBRIETY CHECKPOINT

I once attended a holiday function with a local model. She wasn't famous nationally, but she was locally, and became the life of the party. I enjoyed her company and she certainly appeared to enjoy mine. However, in the corner, I noticed an acquaintance with a bottle of wine. He had removed it from the refreshment area of the banquet hall and was imbibing it liberally. Finally, after an hour or so of drinking, he tossed the bottle and walked over towards us. His speech was slurred and he struggled to stay upright, but he still tried to have a conversation. He started it all by admitting he needed to drink in order to talk to someone so good looking. She was completely turned off by his behavior and told him so several times. Yet, he was too drunk to notice or even care.

Throughout the book, I'll mention bars and clubs a lot. I'm honestly not a huge fan of these places for meeting new people. Why? First, because a lot of people, like my acquaintance in the previous paragraph, use alcohol and other drugs as a social crutch. Second, most people at bars or clubs are trying to project an image of who they want to be, not who they really are. And, everyone knows that. So, everyone's guard is completely up.

What you typically get is desperate guys making fools of themselves, hitting on girls who want nothing to do with them. But, you can't blame the ladies either. They want quality men, but then have to sort through fifteen drunk losers with bad pickup lines just to maybe find one outstanding guy (and, even then, still don't).

In spite of my issues with these establishments, you'll find that I reference bars and clubs frequently throughout the book. I do this because, like it or not, these locations are where a lot of people end up on a Friday or Saturday night. I'm not going to fight the culture on this, but I do want you to be aware of a few things.

First, even if you do go to bars and clubs, I would just view them as training or practice, not a place to make lasting friendships or enduring romances. So, if you feel you have to go, then just practice your techniques. If you can handle the high stress environment of a singles club, then you can meet people anywhere. Then, having trained under the most stressful and negative conditions, when you meet people in your everyday life, the techniques you've learned in this book will be much easier to execute. You might meet someone in a bar or club you really love, but even if you don't, the "practice" mentality keeps you detached (see Chapter 15).

Second, it's important to develop a social life outside of those settings. Hanging out at a bar, especially if you have a reason for being there (watching sports, eating dinner, meeting new people, dancing) is acceptable, but being the guy who never leaves is very low value.

Society is fickle in this regard. It promotes drinking at every turn (just watch all the beer commercials), but judges drunks very harshly. You don't want to be "that guy" known around town for hanging out in a bar all day. Make sure you diversify your environments, not only for social practice, but also to be a healthy, well-rounded person. Visit coffee shops, festivals, religious or civic events, work functions, etc. Being a celebrity means being popular in a variety of places anyway.

Third, bars and clubs are often very loud and chaotic. A lot of the techniques in this book center around showing your high value and winning friends through humor, the use of language manipulation techniques, and building rapport. It's really tough to do that if you can't even hear the person next to you. If you do start at a loud bar and manage to meet someone nice and open, try to move to a different place, like a restaurant or coffee shop where you can actually talk to the person.

Finally, if you do go out to bars and clubs, stay sober. This is for a couple of reasons. Number one, you need to learn and master these techniques and internalize them – without a chemical crutch. For example, approaching strangers can be tough, but it's something you need to do without the help of some liquid courage. Number two, at those places most people are either drunk or at least slightly impaired. If you have your wits, you will be far more successful since you start with an immediate advantage. It's like with my introductory story. I was far more effective in winning over the model than my drunk acquaintance.

If you think you have a problem with drugs or alcohol, don't suffer in silence. You're not alone. Addiction is a disease, meaning that it is something that needs treatment, just like diabetes or a broken bone. Find a community substance abuse agency or an Alcoholics Anonymous meeting in your area and get some help.

Although it may seem like drugs and alcohol can help you be popular in the short term, the long term consequences are usually impaired functioning, decreased quality of life, and an early death. Trust me, the toothless, sore covered meth junkie and the shuffling alcoholic with the look of death in his face are no one's idea of popular or fun. They're just sad.

Your practice for this chapter is to write down a list of venues where you can go out and meet new people. Be specific, writing down their actual names, and include at least three that are not clubs or bars. If you can't think of any venues or any non-bar places, then do some research. Find a place that looks like it would be busy, fun, and match your values. After you do this, list a few of the crutches in your life you use to be at ease with other people. It could be alcohol, being with your outgoing best friend, etc. Once you identify these, try to break away from these a bit and be popular on your own, without the "help."

CHAPTER 5

DO THE BEST RIGHT NOW

"I'll start eating healthily right after I get back from vacation."

"I'll be more generous once I get that raise."

"I'll talk to that girl when I see her in the club...next week."

What do these statements all have in common? They all put off for tomorrow what should be done today! And, you know as well as I do, that, in all three examples, the person who makes those statements will never follow through when the time to act supposedly arrives. In fact, all of these are real examples and, in each case, the people involved never followed up. You see, true change begins right now. This is an important lesson. It's also one that popular and successful people know well.

Since you're just starting this book, you may already find yourself making excuses as to why you can't do the activities I recommend. Maybe you feel that you'll implement them at some point down the line, like when you feel better about yourself or when the conditions are more ideal. Get out of that mindset. Before you even go on to the next paragraph, vow to take the necessary steps to be popular right now.

I once had the opportunity to hear actor Brian Stepanek of Disney's "Suite Life of Zack and Cody" television show speak. He told a great story about how, as a struggling actor, he had the chance to headline his own show in Chicago. He felt that after years of hard work performing in smaller venues outside of the big city that he had at last arrived as an actor. The first night in the windy city he didn't exactly play to a packed house. In fact, he played for an audience of *one*.

He was naturally disheartened and could have easily given up and said "I'll try again in the future." But he didn't. He performed the entire show for that one person with the same passion he would've given a full theater (and the guy even came back after intermission). Stepanek said that he stayed on the stage because he loved what he was doing, and he was never going to give up his dreams. Brian Stepanek did the best he could right then. He knew, like other high value successful people, that you can't wait until the perfect time arrives because the perfect time will never come!

In addition, the successful and popular person knows that if he can't achieve a mental state now (e.g. generosity, happiness, etc.), then it will never happen in the future. The same is true for you. If you can't be fun, happy, cool, witty, and popular in your present environment, then you never will in Hollywood, New York City or anywhere else. It's like teenagers (and adults?) who fantasize about playing guitar in a giant stadium, but can't even get up the nerve to play at their high school talent contest. Here's a hint: if you can't play for fifty, you won't be able to play for fifty thousand!

You must always act like a celebrity in every environment, right now. If you're a college student, then become a celebrity in your Biology 101 class or the dorm. If you work at a small company in Des Moines, then be popular there with the five employees. You'll practice your craft and then, as you become more successful and branch out in life, you'll have the skills to become a celebrity in bigger places and with more people.

As you be the best you can be right now, your brain is rewiring to make you even closer to your best self. Even if you work a boring job at Burger King monitoring the deep fryer, I promise you that angry customers and stressed employees would love to have someone they could laugh with and look up to during a bad day. You can play that role. When you perfect your abilities in front of those five night shift employees and couple hundred customers, then you're ready to branch out to bigger crowds.

There are a variety of issues that keep people from doing the best right now. First, some people can't distinguish between dreams and fantasies. They fantasize about something impossible and can't accept anything short of their wildest imagination. They make the good the enemy of the perfect and never take advantage of the small opportunities necessary to be popular and famous. An example of this could be a talented keyboard player who seems to think he's going to be the next Elton John and refuses to take opportunities to build his music career slowly through smaller venues (which is actually what Elton John did).

Second, a lot of individuals are snobs. Even though they aren't world famous, they still think they have a license to look down on other people. I knew a guy like this in high school. He played football and, although he wasn't very good at it, still walked around like he was the star of the team. Individuals like this seem to think they've already arrived, so they have no need for improvement or growth. They rarely end up popular or successful.

Third, many people are simply lazy. They give new meaning to the crude piece of advice "wish in one hand, crap in the other, and see which one fills up faster." In other words, they hope that all it takes to be popular is wishful thinking and a wing and a prayer. They fail to realize that behind every successful person is someone who worked hard. Successful people held on to their dreams and hopes, for sure. But, they also took the difficult steps and put in the grunt work to make sure they were successful.

You need to avoid these traps if you want to be popular. First, follow your dreams, but don't get caught up in pointless fantasizing. Instead of daydreaming, start working to make your dream a reality. Second, don't look down on anybody. A fan is a fan. If you want a million of them, you have to build them one by one (as Brian Stepanek discovered). Continue to grow and remember, that for all your talents, there's always someone more talented.

Finally, there may be difficult moments on the path to popularity. However, you have to constantly remind yourself of how great you will feel when you achieve popularity. Whenever you are anxious, afraid, or just plain tired of the hard work of personal change, re-read the first part of the book's introduction and imagine yourself living those initial scenarios. Leaving your comfort zone is worth it!

Your practice assignment for this chapter is to simply start doing your best right now. Right now, wherever you are and whatever you're doing, I want you to stop (unless you're doing something essential) and interact positively with another person. Call him, text her, or walk over and see him. Break out of your comfort zone a little (or a lot) and just do it. Write a few sentences about your experience.

Once you've interacted with another person, examine your list of affirmations and declarations and brainstorm ways you will start living your future goals *at this moment*, even though it may be on a much smaller scale. For example, if you chose "I am impacting millions of people" as an affirmation, start impacting the five people who work next to you right now. Then, you can start thinking about the millions.

CHAPTER 6

DON'T JUST BE YOURSELF

While in college, I developed some serious hang-ups and had trouble interacting with really beautiful women. I never knew what to say, was scared to death of rejection, and often spent my spare time free of female company. However, during one night of lonely philosophizing with my male friends, I told one of them that if someone asked me to approach women as a part of an experiment, or if I was ordered to approach a hot woman at gunpoint, I could. In other words, if necessary, I could *act* the part. What I didn't realize then is that while "I" couldn't do it, I pretending to be "someone else," could!

If you're reading this, you're probably an adult. As mentioned in Chapter 3, the older you are, the more likely you are defined by years of brain wiring. Some of this could be positive, like your brain telling you that you're smart. But, you may also have a lot of baggage relating to social situations. Maybe it's that rejection by your crush when you were in fifth grade. Or perhaps it's your college English professor who basically called you a loser in front of the whole class. Most people are bogged down by years of negative self-talk, which their brain happily (and automatically) regurgitates at inopportune times.

You don't have to be handicapped by your faulty brain wiring. And, you can see some significant change immediately. However, don't stop doing your affirmations and declarations just yet. These are essential to long term success. Still, I'm going to share with you a cool secret we developed with our good friend Joshua Wagner: you defeat your negativity by simply not being you. That's right. You create your "avatar," which, in this sense, means the embodiment of your ideal self.

To do this, you first must decide what your goals in life are. You should already have done this when you made your affirmations and declarations. Now, you'll need to take some time to imagine how you would act, look, think, and, most importantly, feel, as your best self. Then, go out and do it. You're no longer (fill in your given name), but a new, dynamic person who lives according to his new values and expectations. Give your avatar a name and make it powerful. You don't have to share it with anyone. Maybe it's Eric Power (or, if you're a female reader, Megan Crusher).

Whenever you are in an environment or situation where you would normally fail or stumble, stop being "you" and morph into your avatar. You may get scared around women, but your avatar dates anyone he pleases. You may be timid around your colleagues at work, but your avatar is a successful businessman who takes names and kicks butt. You get the point.

You may be thinking that this is, in essence, lying to yourself or others. But it's not. The more you act like your avatar (your ideal self), the more you become your avatar. After all, these are your goals which you are constantly working towards. Acting like you're confident, popular, and the hottest guy in the room isn't a lie because that's who you're becoming! You're just speeding up the process by using an avatar.

The temptation may be to lie about the details. Avoid this; you are a celebrity, not a con artist. If you work at McDonald's, don't tell your new friends that you're a successful businessman in food retail. However, if your avatar is a successful entrepreneur, then go out and start a business! Then you can tell others that you're starting a successful business and it's completely true.

If you think this is weird advice, just remember that every popular celebrity has an avatar. You can tell this just by turning on the television. Do you really think Dane Cook is funny all the time or Kim Kardashian looks like a photo-shopped babe first thing in the morning? Of course not! They get into their roles and play up the celebrity aspects of their personalities when the situation dictates. Some celebrities like Alice Cooper (a conservative Republican and Christian) have outrageous avatars who aren't even reflective of their "normal" selves at all.

Right now your real self and your avatar may be miles apart, but that can change quickly by getting out and living like your avatar. If you find it tough, think about the WWJD bands that were a fad in the 90s. They stood for "What Would Jesus Do?" and the idea was that in times of temptation a person could see the band and make choices in line with the philosophy of Jesus. You can ask yourself something similar to bring out your avatar. When you are in a situation that makes you anxious and you're unsure about your popularity instinct, ask yourself, "what would (my avatar) do?"

Once I was out at a festival and a really pretty girl was working at a drink stand. I wanted to say something to her, just to make her laugh. I'm not sure whether it was my old mentality rearing its ugly head, but I became shy while standing in the line, even though I'm married and not even in the dating game! I told myself it wouldn't be the end of the world if I didn't talk to her.

While true about the world not ending, for me, that answer was a huge cop out. So, I asked myself, "What would my avatar do?" I knew that "he" would get this girl laughing. So, I channeled my avatar and talked to her. Sure enough, I got her breaking into laughter as well as the people around her. I found a way to tap into my ideal self at the right moment by invoking my avatar. And, approaching strangers, even pretty women, became that much easier after that day, so the distance between my avatar and me shortened.

I want to say a little bit about what an avatar is not so you don't get the wrong idea. It's not your childhood fantasy, your superhero dream, or anything unobtainable or utterly impractical. If you're forty-five and never picked up a guitar, your avatar can't be a guitar hero playing Wembley (I don't care if you play "Guitar Hero" daily). Your avatar is your best self, not a comic book character, pipe dream, or some obscure character from Star Wars you always wished you could be. If you get any desires to dress as a superhero and go out in public, skip to Chapter 20 immediately!

Your practice for this chapter has two parts. The first assignment is to craft your avatar. With your affirmations and declarations, you should have an idea of who you want to be. Now you're creating the "embodiment" of those goals. Write down how your avatar dresses, acts, and talks. With whom does he associate? How does he respond in difficult situations? Where does your avatar spend his time? I want you to provide some details because every aspect of your life should be defined by your new goals.

Next, armed with your descriptions, I want you to go out and live like your avatar for a night. Go to a coffee shop, club, mall, or anywhere with lots of people. And, when you're there, give yourself permission to act as your avatar. Ask yourself "what would (my avatar) do?" frequently. Then, just do it. If you're a little worried about the results, give yourself permission to be your avatar for a few hours at first. I think you'll find that being your best self is easy and even fun, probably much more fun than spending a night being "you."

CHAPTER 7

FLEXIBILITY TRAINING

Back when I was a teacher, one year my colleagues and I were asked, as a department, to come up with several goals for the next school year. We did this in April. Once August hit, we started to implement those goals during our weekly Monday staff meetings. However, by October, our needs had changed, so we asked the assistant principal if we could change our goals. To our shock, we were told "no." So, for the next nine months of the school year, we wasted nearly every Monday session pointlessly working on outdated goals while our real needs continued to be unmet. We were held hostage by a half page goal sheet and an inflexible bureaucrat.

If the above example seems ridiculous, then at least you have some common sense. However, I'm sure your life has its share of inflexibility too. Perhaps you have some routine or habit that you either won't break or can't break, even if you know it's unhelpful. Likely, if you're not as popular as you'd like to be, you have some inflexibility in social situations and relationships as well.

But, if you want to be popular, then you must also be flexible and adaptable. Whatever your situation or environment, you must assess it, act, then constantly adapt as the situation requires. If you think back to science class, such adaptation is the foundation for the existence of all life. Sadly, not every species has managed. Those that failed are no longer on this planet. Don't become "socially" extinct because you can't adapt.

The best and most successful people are completely adaptable and flexible. During the 2011 season of "Celebrity Apprentice," musician John Rich was a finalist, along with actress Marlee Matlin. Rich had scheduled a concert with 80s glam metal band Def Leppard to promote his business project. On the day of the concert, he went in front of the rather large crowd and announced the coming of Def Leppard to great fanfare and cheers. He was greeted by an empty stage and a roadie telling him that he got the time wrong.

Now, most people simply would've given up, convinced they had already lost the competition. Perhaps a small minority would regain some composure, but stumble to a second place finish. Doubtlessly, a few would completely melt down and become a laughingstock in the annals of reality TV (and among reality show participants being a laughingstock takes a lot).

Not John Rich. He behaved like a successful man and a true celebrity. He apologized for the mix-up, then started performing his own songs. In essence, he became the warm-up act for Def Leppard. And, guess what? Thanks to his flexibility, the audience was able to hear two famous artists that night. Not only that, but he probably went away with thousands of new fans, especially after the episode aired on television. Honestly, I'd never even paid attention to the guy until watching TV that night!

A hard and rigid tree won't survive a storm; a flexible one will.

Being flexible is often a matter of personality and, from my experience, can be somewhat hard to teach to naturally rigid people. However, the guiding principle for flexibility is to relax and stop taking yourself so seriously. The people who have the hardest time adapting are those who are too rigid to let go. I'm always amazed at how tenaciously people hold to ideas, time-frames, stereotypes, and even their image of themselves, when life seems to be screaming: "Adapt for goodness sake!"

If you are naturally a little rigid and want to increase your flexibility, try to get into a flexible mentality and then make your daily choices based on that perspective. If the restaurant is out of your favorite coffee, remember a flexible person will try the other blend, not throw a fit. If your colleague has to cancel an appointment, it's not the end of the world. I think you get the idea. If you know someone who is adaptable and relaxed, model that person. You'll see how flexibility looks on a daily basis in the real world.

Being flexible typically involves a lot of re-framing (see Chapter 3 for review). You'll have to look at events and people according to different frames of reference. This may not be easy because you've developed a lot of habits and entrenched viewpoints. For example, my former boss couldn't fathom changing a goal mid-year. She could've easily re-framed the situation if she let herself. But she just couldn't, for whatever reason.

If you really are intent on becoming a celebrity, you must always be ready to adapt, especially in social situations. You are going to learn certain techniques in this book like using humor, recovering from setbacks, approaching people, etc. And I can tell you these techniques are not always successful. They work most of the time, but when they don't, you'll have to pick up your ego, move on, and try something else that does work. This is flexibility in action. If you find yourself being anxious and inflexible, immediately re-frame the situation so that you can instead be popular and happy. It's not always easy, but it is possible.

In addition, as you become more popular, jealous people will be watching you to see how you behave when you encounter bumps in the road. Look at how the public pounces when a big name celebrity disgraces himself. It's not pretty! While you likely won't experience such vitriol, chances are good that once you become popular there will be people who will root for you to fail. Flexibility ensures that there will never really be true failure (more on this in Chapter 11).

Your assignment is now to add being flexible and adaptable to your affirmations and declarations. I challenge you to really make being flexible a priority in your life. Next, you'll need to go out and practice your new, flexible perspective on a daily basis. If you are naturally uptight, this is essential. However, even those of us who are pretty flexible sometimes need a reminder in stressful situations.

CHAPTER 8

GIVE, GET, AND GIVE (MORE)

I grew up in a small town where almost everyone knew each other. One of the local celebrities was a successful business owner. Although he didn't advertise it, he was very generous in helping people, especially when they fell on hard times. He gave generously, without expecting anything in return. However, as a good businessman, he knew that he actually would receive something in return: the loyalty of the people he helped. When they were back on their feet, they gave him their business, even if his prices were a little higher. Of course, the more business he received, the more he was able to help even more people down the line.

He embodied a principle that we developed (along with Joshua

Wagner) called the "give-get-give" cycle. Like many of the tips in this book, it's not just a trait of popular people, but also very successful ones. No one becomes successful and famous without first giving of themselves. I'm not talking about charity here, although the give-get-give cycle should include that at some point.

Let's look at successful businessmen and women, athletes and musicians. They don't become wealthy because people randomly give away money to them. No, these famous people give the masses something they want, like a gizmo, service, or even entertainment. It's what MJ DeMarco, in his book <u>Millionaire Fastlane</u>, calls the "law of effection." The more people you impact, the more money and success you will ultimately have. You give, you get. Then you give some more and get some more. By the way, if you want to find financial success (and you should because this helps make you even more popular), starting reading DeMarco's book alongside this one. You won't regret it.

This is the concept that gets me, and other popular people like me, free stuff. It's not just a matter of "this guy is popular around here" so he gets a free coffee, a first class upgrade, or something else of value. Rather, I am on the receiving end of generosity because I give others something they value, such as a chance to laugh, entertainment, networking opportunities, or maybe just time with someone cool when they've been dealing with jerks all day. They, out of appreciation, reward me in whatever way they can. Giving back because you receive something first is what <u>Influence</u> author Robert Cialdini calls "reciprocity" and humans have a strong instinct to give back once they have received a gift. I would highly recommend Cialdini's book as supplemental reading in addition to DeMarco's.

One summer, while traveling, I went to a Caribou Coffee I'd never visited before. I walked in with my brother and we started some of our humor routines (see Chapter 14). After interacting with the sales girl for a little while (and getting a free iced coffee), she told us that we made her day because, get this, she NEVER encounters people like us on a daily basis. We gave her a good time in the midst of a normally boring and frustrating day, and we got a free coffee out of the deal. I would argue, however, that she got more value. A good day is worth far more than a two-dollar coffee.

Getting in the give-get-give mindset can be tough. We're used to thinking in terms of scarcity. In other words, we think we can't give something away because we're afraid it won't be reciprocated. So, people become cheap with money and time and aren't generous to others for fear of being taken advantage of or getting nothing in return. That attitude has to go if popularity is your goal.

Give of your best self all the time and be generous with your money and time. If you're low on money, then just give of yourself. If you truly touch a multitude of people, then your generosity will come back to you in spades.

If you're still in doubt, look at Google. They give away the vast, vast majority of their services, yet make more money than most other companies on the planet. Their give-get-give mindset has made their owners billionaires. I guarantee that if Google hoarded their services and nickeled and dimed consumers for all of them, they probably wouldn't even be around today.

Give-get-give means you give more, but also get more…and then give more!

A great example of someone who gives of himself is my friend and athlete Roy W. Hall. A wide receiver with the Ohio State Buckeyes and then the Indianapolis Colts and Detroit Lions, Hall has certainly had a good taste of fame and celebrity, especially since he was a part of the National Championship Ohio State team in 2002.

Roy gave of his talents to the Ohio State Buckeyes in a sport that requires lots of time and bodily abuse. The fans, in return for his hard work and success, gave him their love, support, and admiration. After he retired from the NFL, Roy, a smart, articulate, and passionate guy dedicated to his family and his Christian faith, started giving back to the Columbus community through his D.R.I.V.E.N. Foundation. It is dedicated to providing educational programming along with support services to underserved communities throughout Central Ohio and surrounding cities. His charity work not only helps others, but also increases his networking contacts and impact on the community. Thus, he continues to "get" new opportunities as well. He is a perfect example of give-get-give at work. You can support D.R.I.V.E.N. by going to http://drivenfoundation.org/ and follow Roy on Twitter under the handle @Roy_Hall.

The hardest part of give-get-give is to take that first step and actually give. When we have something of value, it's very tough to give it away. However, with time, ideas, and talents, it's absolutely essential that we share them with the world if we ever want to see anything (like money, fame, or the joy of helping others) given to us in return.

Your assignment is to list your talents and think of ways you can give them to the world. Don't worry about how you're going to "get" in return at this stage. If you have something genuine to offer the world, and give it abundantly, you will receive more back than you know what to do with.

CHAPTER 9

MAJOR LEAGUES

When I was in middle school, I had a huge crush on Stacy. She was not only incredibly good looking to my preteen self, but she was smart, her family had a ton of money, and she was a model for local companies. She was my perfect woman! In fifth grade, I sent Stacy a note during one English class and she actually passed one back. I couldn't believe it. We even talked on the phone over the next few days. I could barely contain my excitement at having a chance with the cutest girl in the fifth grade.

That's when my "friend" informed me, in a very stressed voice, that Stacy was smart, rich, and gorgeous. He said it twice to show me he meant business. When I didn't get his obvious point (because I knew how great she was), he explained it in easier terms: she was out of my league. She would, he figured, only go out with demigods like herself. Mere mortals like he and I shouldn't bother. I took his foolish words to heart, got nervous, and stopped talking to Stacy. Even though she was cool to me, I let my supposed friend talk me out of an opportunity for a cute girlfriend, or at least a new friend. And, it was in spite of the evidence I saw with my own eyes (and heard with my own ears), that she actually liked me!

You can look at other people in two ways. The first is the "leagues" view that my friend believed: people are categorized into levels, from easily obtainable to "out of my league" (e.g. that guy's tall and handsome; he won't want to be my friend" or "that hot girl would never date me"). This view creates a pecking order and implies that popular, successful, and beautiful people are somehow radically different from the rest of us. We put them on a pedestal and consider ourselves unworthy to associate with them. This is the common position and it will keep you from being a happy person. Trust me.

The second view sees others in terms of "types." People can be in preferred or non-preferred categories (e.g. nerd, jock, ditzy blonde, etc.) and you may prefer one to another for friends, dating, business, etc. But, with the types perspective, no person is off limits simply because she is too successful, too cool or too anything. This is how successful individuals view the world.

Think about the issue for a minute. A person can be a poor sap living in a shack and yet be a jerk and a snob who wants nothing to do with you. On the other hand, a successful businessman who lives in a mansion may be a genuinely amazing guy who wants to be your friend and help you in incredible ways. By thinking in terms of leagues, you are limiting your chances at success and you will never be popular. Looking at people in terms of types is different. It makes you in charge of your destiny. No one is too good or "too anything" for you. You are only limited by your own desire to limit interaction.

Of course, I also want you to be realistic. Some people will be more difficult to win over and are naturally less accessible. The CEO of a big company may have less time than your neighbor who works 9-5 as a tech guy. However, the CEO still may be a cool, open person whom you can win over with your skills. And, imagine the reward of winning over someone of that caliber. Most people would defeat themselves from the start by not even trying. However, you know the CEO (or the beautiful model or anyone) is just another type of person you can impress, not an unapproachable guy or girl that is out of your league.

If it makes you feel better, many people in power, if they remember their roots, are actually pretty cool. They became popular and famous because they were excellent at relating to people. Granted, some people made it to the top because they were ruthless and played the game better than anyone else. These individuals may not be fun to deal with, but they're also not out of anyone's league. They're just a bigger challenge. Everyone has basic needs, even the most powerful people and the biggest jerks. A confident, popular person should be able to positively influence anyone in any situation because he has learned the right tools to win over everyone.

However, don't use your recognition of "types" to limit yourself either. Mentally admitting that you never approach certain "types" due to the challenges they present is just excuse making in action. A client once told me he doesn't like the hot, confident "type" of woman because they're too hard to approach and win over. That's just "league" thinking using different language! Also, don't get so caught up in putting people into types that you close yourself off to a diverse group of people. For example, if you only prefer to deal with a limited number of types, you're going to limit your overall popularity.

It's going to take a little while to get used to thinking differently about people. We are accustomed to creating a little hierarchy among ourselves. However, you know better. And the "types" way of thinking gives you access to anyone and everyone, whatever their position on the supposed totem pole. It's what makes a true celebrity. After all, a superstar has fans from the allegedly beautiful people down to the supposed dregs.

Your assignment for this chapter is to believe that there are types, not leagues. But, before you get off too easily, I want you to go out to a club, mall, or other busy venue and find a person that, if you believed in hierarchies (and you don't), would be the most intimidating person in the place. I want you to go and talk to that man or woman. Just be friendly and strike up a conversation.

I want you to notice a couple of things. One, the popular person really is human, just like you, and may actually be pretty cool. Two, even if he or she isn't interested in you, it's not the end of your world to find out that fact. You may even make a nice connection. Just don't blow it like I did with Stacy all those years ago by not even trying.

CHAPTER 10

EVERYONE IS PRACTICE

In college, I traveled to South Carolina with a good friend and his family for a summer vacation. One evening, while we were walking to the car from a nice seafood restaurant, his father noticed that my brother and I didn't smile at a girl we passed. He asked us why and we told him we didn't think she was that pretty. Doc, a master of the female mind, even at seventy (seriously), told us that ugly girls needed love too.

His response really stuck with me and is closely related to the "types, not leagues" thinking from the last chapter. It helped me learn an important tenet for having a successful social life: in whatever your popularity goals, everyone is practice. Not only would it have been a nice gesture to smile at that girl, it actually would've also helped me with something I was horrible at in college...smiling at girls! That's right, if I couldn't or wouldn't smile at a homely girl hundreds of miles from home, how could I smile at the hot number at the student union in my town? The answer: I couldn't. And didn't.

For someone wanting to be popular, this is a very important chapter and is intimately connected to the previous advice of "do the best now." Being a celebrity involves being liked by all kinds of people. Do you think just the beautiful people watch Brad Pitt movies? Are only supermodels among the throngs of fans wanting to see Justin Bieber? Nope. And if you only won over hot women and handsome men, you wouldn't have enough fans to even be popular.

So, everyone you encounter is practice. Everyone. You treat everyone like a potential fan in the making. That guy on the treadmill who talks too much? Get him telling others about how awesome you are! The teenager with zits who works down at Burger King? Make her one of your adoring fans. The crabby lady who cleans the offices at work? Be the only one who can make her laugh.

If you do this, you'll truly get what popular people have by definition: fans. And these fans will go to bat for you and help you if necessary. Maybe the guy jiggling on the treadmill owns a tire shop and can get you a great, honest deal. The zit covered teen at Burger King? How about giving you a discount each time you visit? And that angry old lady at work? Maybe she has a really cute daughter.

When everyone is practice, you win big. You get to hone your craft as an emerging celebrity and build your fan base. In addition, people get to know you, which, if you're following this book, should bring a little more joy and fun to a world that needs it. Besides, as Brian Stepanek knows, your fan base begins with the number "one." And you build it fan by fan. Unless you have a break-out album, or are a freaky talented athlete, you have to work rooms, make connections, and charm the pants off everyone you meet (especially that cute girl). You do that by making sure everyone is practice.

Your assignment for this chapter is simple. Go out tonight and interact with everyone you encounter. You don't have to talk to *everyone* you see because that could be a little creepy. But, you should at least smile or say "hi" to the people who pass in your general direction. And, I want you to talk to at least five people. And treat everyone the same. Don't let the beautiful girl scare you off, and don't thumb your nose at the fat guy working the hot dog stand.

Chapter 11

No Failure, Only Feedback

A college basketball coach, I think it was John Wooden, had a film assistant who accidentally deleted an entire game film. The unlucky man went to Coach Wooden and apologized, fully expecting to be fired. Wooden asked him if he knew his mistake and if he learned from it. The film guy answered in the affirmative to both questions. Wooden told him not to make the mistake again, but kept him on staff. This story illustrates an important point: a mistake is not a failure, if it results in feedback.

Any popular person knows that failure is not in his vocabulary. Sure, what happens may look like failure to an outside observer, but anyone who is successful and driven views it as only a temporary setback and a valuable chance to receive feedback. Of course, he does this with the goal of not repeating the mistake again.

As you work your way into fame and popularity, you will be like a child finding his identity. Although I believe strongly in this book and its techniques, you are not one of the authors. You'll have to find your own way. And it will involve some huge successes, but also some pretty major "failure." And my flexibility advice from Chapter 7? It's golden. But, sorry boy (or girl), you're only human. Sometimes you just won't be able to adapt quickly enough or adapt at all. You'll inevitably experience what some people term "failure."

When something doesn't go as you would have liked it, you have two options. The first option is to let the supposed failure cripple you. This can happen if you dwell on it, get depressed over it, claim it's someone else's fault, or live in denial, assuring yourself it was actually a success. Most people react in one of these ways. They do not perform at a task in the way they wanted and either give up in depression, or stubbornly continue moving forward using the same ineffective methods.

You could be like everyone else and either give up or persist on an unsuccessful path, but guess where it'll get you? I can assure you it's not a life of success. For one, if you're throwing your lot with the majority, then I hate to break it to you: the majority work lousy jobs they hate, are constantly stressed, live in loneliness, and are not popular. You are different. You will be taking the second option.

Your response will be to learn from your "failure." Notice the quotes. When you learn from your mistakes, you don't even really experience failure. Some banks and state governments are more likely to approve business loans to those who have failed once before. Why? Because those businesspeople already (we hope) learned from their mistakes. And, people who see each and every mistake as an opportunity for feedback (whether from self or others) are much less likely to make mistakes of any sort in the future.

As I mentioned previously, I worked as a school teacher before I started my own business. I was very successful with all my students, but ran into problems with bureaucratic leadership. In spite of massive student and parent protests, my contract was not renewed.

I could've stewed in resentment at the injustice and let that feeling guide my future. I also could've applied for more teaching jobs and possibly endured the same treatment with another administrator. I was even tempted to enter "corporate America" and try my hand there. But a good friend had the guts to tell me the truth about where a former teacher would start. At the bottom, of course, dealing with micromanaging bosses and the same nonsense I hated as a teacher!

Rather than repeat the same mistake, I looked for other options and found a way to not let anyone else determine my future: I started my own business. It's been hard work, but I'm building something I love and doing it on my own terms. Instead of accepting the alleged failure of losing my job and letting it destroy me, I turned it into a blessing. I looked at my own life critically (in the positive sense of self-reflection) and heeded the advice of friends and colleagues. What could've been a crushing vocational defeat or a sideways jump to more misery, ended up being a giant leap forward as I pursue my passion of teaching others how to be popular.

If you fall flat on your face and still want to be a success, you must immediately ask what you may have done wrong and learn from it. Actually, let me correct that last statement. *When* you fall flat on your face... However, with each lesson learned, you'll be honing your craft as a popular man, getting closer and closer to being the person you want to be.

Right now I'd like you to make a list of major events in your life that didn't end up as you intended. Maybe it was a relationship that soured, a lost job, a bad financial decision, etc.

This exercise may be painful, but it's important to complete if you want to move forward. Then, for each mistake you've listed, I want you to come up with a couple of lessons that you've learned. If you haven't really learned a lesson from a major "failure," then I urge you to think long and hard about how to avoid that mistake in the future. You definitely don't want to go down an unsuccessful path more than once!

However, you also don't want to dwell on your previous mistakes to the point that you are crippled by your past. Almost every major celebrity has a project, album, movie, or sports performance they wish they could forget. However, that didn't stop their careers from taking off. You should always learn from your mistakes, but don't focus too much on the mistakes themselves. This is Chapter 11 for a reason. Learn from your mistakes, then start over! With everything in life, there is no failure, only feedback.

CHAPTER 12

ETHICS OF POPULARITY 101

Brandon Flowers is the lead singer of "The Killers," a popular band with many hit albums and singles. Known for his large vocal range, songwriting talent, and good looks, Flowers lives the life of a celebrity. While his songs are loved by millions of people, very few of them know that Flowers is an active member of the Mormon Church and that his faith is a major part of his life. In fact, some of the earliest supporters of the Killers were Flowers' Mormon friends. The themes of faith and family are evident in the lyrics he writes as well. In short, he's popular and sticks to his values.

I've been mentioning a lot about writing affirmations, creating new brain wiring, living as your best self, treating everyone the same, and so on. Most of you are likely wondering what this has to do with being popular. These topics form the foundation for a new you, so be patient. Some of you, perhaps all of you, are also thinking "This scientific and spiritual stuff doesn't sound anything like the celebrities I know." And you're perfectly justified given the bad behavior of some of the overpaid, under-intelligent idiots who can dunk a basketball or carry a tune, but have no sense of decency. Lindsay Lohan and her ilk are certainly celebrities, but they're not the type that this book wants to create.

I am concerned with creating popular, fun, famous (in whatever their setting) people, not entitled jerks. The best "celebrities" throughout history are those who bless others with their talents and, in some way, give back to the community. Look at the surveys of the most admired people. Every year, they consistently include Mother Theresa, Martin Luther King, Jr., Gandhi, and even Ronald Reagan and Oprah Winfrey. These people all had (or have) values and changed the world for the better. These examples were not only beloved and popular, but highly influential. Millions of people were changed for the better thanks to Mother Theresa and Martin Luther King, Jr. On the other hand, in twenty years (maybe even two), the question will be "Lindsay who?"

Perhaps you just want to be a fame whore. If so, you wouldn't be alone. In that case, you probably don't need this chapter or even the book. Anyone can be famous in some fashion for a short period of time. Andy Warhol noted in the future everyone will have fifteen minutes of fame. A good example of Warhol's prophecy is "Angelyne," an 80's "celebrity" who became slightly famous for putting up a billboard of herself in Los Angeles followed by some self-promotion. I wouldn't call her a real celebrity, but more of a glorified attention seeker. Today (and even in the 80's) she was only a curiosity. Also, serial killers become famous and make the news. However, they're not popular and beloved. If you want to be a celebrity for the ages, one who is remembered and loved, then you will need to have ethics.

The first and most basic rule of celebrity ethics is to simply follow your own value system. Unless you were raised by wolves, you should have a basic sense of right and wrong. Follow that and don't sell out to be popular. If you are a strong Christian, then find a way to be popular while staying true to your faith. If you love animals and value their rights, then don't join the circus just to get some added attention. However, don't be obnoxious about your positions either. Outspoken celebrities like Alec Baldwin and Mel Gibson have lost fans over the years, not due to their political and religious values, but because they use them as a weapon to disparage others and create division.

Second, and this rule is in addition to your chosen values, leave others better off after meeting you. Everyone has an experience of meeting famous people. If they were cool and obliging towards your attention, chances are you were on cloud nine after the encounter. That's because meeting famous people typically leaves us feeling happy and excited. This is what you should aim for in your encounters. Your goal as a popular person is to make people feel better about themselves and liven up their day a little. This is in contrast to some so-called celebrities who leave a trail of destruction in their wake.

For example, when I was an undergraduate in college, a popular filmmaker visited my college campus. The students excitedly opened up to him, but he was so critical and bitter towards them that pretty much everybody left the event hating both the experience and the filmmaker himself. Don't let this be you, because you won't be beloved for very long if you act like him. In fact, I don't think this filmmaker has had a hit movie in the last decade. I'm not really surprised.

The third rule is to include, rather than exclude. A truly popular person is always looking to widen his fan base. Consequently, you don't want to mock others, be a bully, or do something that would otherwise make people hate you. I knew a guy in middle school who was really popular with his very small crowd, but his bullying antics made sure he was hated by much, much larger numbers of people. Sadly, the adult world isn't really all that different. You can stand up for yourself and assert your opinions in ways that don't alienate others (see Chapter 18).

The final rule is another simple one: be cool to people. Don't be the tattletale, the nitpicker, the jerk, the gossiper, the whiner, the troublemaker, the snoop, etc. I was talking to my friends the other day about how awesome it is to encounter truly cool people, the ones who are relaxed and don't give others grief all the time. People like this are always popular (think about the term "cool" and what a great compliment it is). It's because genuinely cool people are so rare. You become one of the cool people and you'll be on your way to guaranteed popularity.

If ever in doubt, a good guideline for celebrity behavior is the golden rule given by Jesus: do to others as you would have them do to you. Many thinkers before Jesus phrased the rule differently: do to others what they do to you. Jesus modified it in an important way. In the old system, if someone treated you like crap, then you repaid the favor and treated them like crap in return.

With the golden rule, you treat the other person positively. This is important because, as a popular guy, you must rise above the nonsense and the negativity. In each situation you encounter, think about how you wished others treated you and act on that impulse rather than continuing the drama.

For this chapter, I'd like to you to write down a list of your core values and reflect on how these will help you or hinder you in becoming popular. How can your values increase your fan base? Think of the example of Brandon Flowers from the first paragraph when coming up with your own answers. Like him, you can use your values and your connections to become popular and beloved too, without having to sell out in the process.

CHAPTER 13

LAUGHTER IS THE BEST MEDICINE (FOR UNPOPULARITY)

Since I like to mix things up a lot, just to keep a little excitement in my life, one day my brother and I drove an hour just to have coffee and work on our business ventures in unfamiliar surroundings. When we went up to order our coffee, we put the charm on the sweet and outgoing teenage employee. She told us if we needed a refill to make sure to ask for her since her colleague, who was on break, was incredibly mean. In fact, this young lady told us that she'd never once, in months of working, had a good encounter with her fellow employee!

So, liking a challenge, David and I made sure to get our refills when this lady returned from break. She had gray hair and looked a little rougher around the edges and, sure enough, she didn't exactly greet us with a smile. Instead of being scared or offended, we started treating her like we did everyone else, telling jokes and being friendly. It took her awhile but she cracked a smile, then chuckled, and finally began laughing. As we were leaving, she stopped cleaning up and told us to have a safe trip. The teenage employee was outside emptying the trash and asked us how we'd gotten the older lady to be so nice. She may have been expecting a different, more esoteric answer, but we told her our pretty ordinary secret weapon: humor.

Laughter has been shown through various scientific studies to have many health benefits. It lowers stress, increases immune response, and decreases blood pressure. It also releases endorphins, the hormones that make us happy (3). In addition, it's hard to be angry, resentful, fearful, or generally negative while laughing. Humor gives us a good feeling and that's what most of us really want!

In spite of the obvious benefits of laughter, most people don't get nearly enough of it. Some sources claim children generally laugh three hundred times in one day (4). While there's no scientific verification, it certainly fits with my observations: my toddler is almost always laughing and smiling, unless that is, an adult tells her to be serious, which seems to occur with greater frequency the older she gets. Sources also put the average adult experience of laughter at only around twenty times a day (4). Sadly, this also fits with my observations. It's also no shock that most adults are walking stress bombs.

However, from my experience, I don't think most adults want such little humor in their lives. It's just the way we've been conditioned to think through years of an educational system and a society that emphasize seriousness and "growing up" to the exclusion of creativity and fun. We probably all have a story where a humorless teacher or authority figure tried to snatch our sense of humor away. Take work, too. How many people actually laugh at work? Chances are that even those who laugh at work have been told more than once to "cool it" because work is supposed to be a serious place. We as a culture "seriously" need to get over ourselves!

As a celebrity you can benefit from this humor challenged, yet laughter needy, society by bringing levity to the world. If I had to pick one, and only one, trait that has made me popular wherever I go, it would be my humor. If I didn't consistently make people genuinely laugh in most circumstances, I would never have achieved the celebrity status in my social circles.

However, one of the reasons that more adults don't laugh is that most people simply aren't funny. Delivering jokes and coming up with funny material is a true art and not everyone is close to being blessed with the skills. Also, most would-be comedians simply repeat stale sketches from television or YouTube hoping no one will ever know they don't have an original bone in their body.

Researchers who have studied humor (yes there are people who pursue this cool area of study) have looked at what makes humor effective on an evolutionary level. The first aspect of successful humor they discovered is incongruity (5). If something is incongruent, it "doesn't fit." This could be anything from a joke that has no punch line to a picture of a dog wearing glasses. A good example is a sketch from the British show "Trigger Happy TV" where a couple of guys in the comedy troupe dress up in cute animal outfits and then "beat up" fellow human cast members. It's funny because the image of a giant, cuddly squirrel bashing a human is extremely incongruent.

It sounds kind of abstract at first, but you can use incongruity to great effect in your daily interactions. It's one of my favorite ways to make people laugh. For example, I use a tip I learned from Joshua Wagner and inject (pardon the pun) drug related humor into the conversation. I'll order a coffee with cream, sweetener, and meth. Most people do a double take, then break into laughter. It's very incongruent because, first of all, it's not a typical coffee order. The incongruity is increased by the fact that I am a total health nut with a fit body, clear skin, and great teeth who has never even tried an illegal drug. If I were an obvious methamphetamine junkie, then such a coffee order would be congruent and an occasion for sadness or revulsion, not humor. Please note: drugs are bad. Being incongruent means you must NOT do drugs for this joke to be funny. Got it?

The second aspect of successful humor is safety, which simply means that the person hearing the joke feels secure. Humor originally may have functioned as a way for humans to relax after a stressful event (6). Once the danger had passed, people could laugh about the situation. It's why we find other people getting scared (like when someone jumps out of a closet) funny, but only from the comfort of our living rooms. If a total stranger were really in our closet, it wouldn't be funny at all. Even if it were a joke, in the moment, it would still be scary and we couldn't laugh until we settled down and realized it was a joke. The squirrel beating up the human is a great example of safety as well. Clearly if a real giant squirrel were pummeling a guy on the street (or even a guy in a costume really beating up someone), it would be a cause for panic. Yet, from a vantage point of security, it's quite funny.

When using humor in public, you must always keep safety in mind. This doesn't mean that since someone is not being eaten by a bear, you can assume she's safe and unleash your humor. The issue of safety is why, I believe, inappropriate humor is disliked by large parts of the population. Simply put, jokes about race, violence, and sex will take away the feeling of safety for many people because these topics have caused them pain in the past (or could). So, obviously, if you are trying to win people over, you should be very, very careful about using dark or edgy humor, especially around people you don't know.

Another important way to be funny is to use situational or observational humor. This is adapting your jokes to current situations. For example, if you are walking through the park, situational humor would find ways to be funny based around what you encounter in the park. This type of humor is beneficial because it has to be original and it makes you look intelligent and quick on your feet, both high value traits. Situational humor can also be based around current events. Once again, using information found in the news or popular culture proves that you pay attention and are intelligent.

Once David and I used a mix of safety, incongruity, and situational humor for great effect with a girl we know. She asked what was in my brief case. She knew it was probably a computer and was trying to be funny. I told her my machine guns are in there. She laughed and told me "yeah right." I then asked her if she'd heard of the trade in body parts from executed Chinese prisoners in the news. She gave me a horrified look and said no. I stared at my briefcase and asked "know anyone who needs a kidney?" She (and the girl nearby) burst into laughter.

That example shows not only a mix of the three types of humor, but also is a little dark and edgy. It pushes some boundaries and you may not even find it funny at all. However, I knew the girls well enough and delivered the joke in a way to pull it off. Sure, it was a gamble, but it paid off big time because it made me look smart and very original. In fact, both girls still jokingly ask me if I have any more body parts for sale. When you are trying material, you have to decide if you think an edgier approach is worth the risk.

Two other types of humor you may want to consider using are anti-humor and the shaggy dog story. They are very similar and I have found both of these very effective in my years of winning fans.

Anti-humor is telling a story or a joke that is so purposefully unfunny that it elicits laughter from the person listening. The earlier example of putting meth in coffee is anti-humor at work. Meth abuse is not a traditionally funny topic (for good reason). Sometimes when we first use the "joke," the employees will give us a bewildered look.

However, once they realize we are kidding (and not real meth users), they start to laugh. However, notice there is no real joke or punch line.

A shaggy dog story is a long, pointless story, usually with ridiculous details and an absurd conclusion. These can be especially effective if delivered with a straight face. For example, once when David and I were at a water park, we were telling a girl about how before I lost a bunch of weight I got stuck in one of the slides and they had to use the jaws of life to get me out. And, I celebrated my rescue with a giant ham dinner. Remember that shaggy dog stories work best with incongruity, so you must make sure that if you're telling an alleged story about yourself that it is incongruent with your personality or other traits. In my example, I was shirtless at a water park, so she could tell I was in great shape. The story was totally BS and everyone knew it. But, for my listeners, it was like being sucked into a brief, funny fantasy.

Just remember when trying to be humorous, that doing something for shock value is rarely funny. In addition, humor is one area where it's possible to be very creepy (see Chapter 20). Telling jokes about inappropriate topics can make others extremely uncomfortable, especially if you generally look and act like a weirdo. I could get away with the Chinese execution joke because I'm a well-dressed professional. A guy with a bunch of piercings, a mohawk, and black, ripped clothing would probably be more believable than incongruent!

Finally, use your judgment to determine when to be funny. I knew a guy who actually walked into a gathering of mourning relatives and started doing his shtick. Needless to say, they tossed him out of the house (quite literally) and he lost several friends. Know when it's time to be funny and when a more serious demeanor is appropriate. In spite of this advice, I still believe humor is appropriate in probably ninety-five percent of situations, even if some uptight person who thinks life is about suffering constantly tells you otherwise. Nonetheless, be aware of the five percent.

For your practice assignment, I'd like you to get on YouTube or get some DVDs and watch a few hours of great comedians. I'd recommend successful ones like Richard Pryor, Eddie Murphy, Chris Rock, and Dane Cook. You can also read funny articles or stories. Cracked.com has some excellent material. These should give you an idea of how humor works and how to tell stories, deliver punch lines, etc. If you know a funny person, then go out and watch him in action. I'd advise watching someone of the same sex since men and women often have different ways of being funny. Take mental notes and see how he elicits laughter. Finally, begin to think about what types of humor you would be most comfortable using. In the next chapter, you'll start coming up with actual material.

CHAPTER 14

MAKE IT ROUTINE

When I went to the gym to play basketball in high school, I would always see one of my classmates there. She was always practicing three point shots. It turns out she wasn't just there when I played (which was fairly rare), but all the time, always practicing those threes. One day I asked her why she practiced so much. She told me that by learning and practicing the best shooting mechanics, she knew that she would be able to sink threes during games without a second thought. In other words, three point shooting would become routine.

The same is true of properly delivering funny material. Although improv comedy is popular, it's not the norm. Most comedians have routines that they write, practice, and then adapt over time. This is because they will always have the best material (and the right amount of it) for all their shows. Although you may not be appearing live at the Apollo, you still should have a large repertoire of funny stories, lines, and other material that you can effortlessly whip out from your brain at a moment's notice.

From a comedy standpoint, a routine is just a series of funny stories, lines, jokes, etc. They are not one off comments or jokes, but sustained attempts at being funny for a longer period of time. The best comedian's routines will effortlessly shift from theme to theme and stack jokes, lines, and stories so that the audience remains captivated for the entire show. When you go out and meet new people, you'll want to have enough routines to keep people laughing and enjoying your presence for as long as you're with them.

When making routines, you have three options: make your own, find someone else's, or a create mixture of the two. I would advise that in the beginning you pick option three and eventually move on to just making your own. I would never recommend using someone else's routines unchanged. They can be very unnatural because they don't reflect your life situation. Not only that, but if you're simply using memorized material, it will become too much like pickup lines. And people hate pickup lines because the only skill they require is memorizing something that you read on the internet.

My advice is to first find some general humor routines on the internet. You should've already looked up comedians on YouTube, but you can also search for websites that specialize in creating funny material. Then, practice doing the routines, adapting them to your personality and your interests. It's key that if you use other people's material as a base that you make it your own. For example, if you never fly and you use a routine about flying on an airplane, the follow-up will be awkward.

Second, you'll have to actually go out and practice the routines. I recommend that you practice with family and friends first. You'll find out what works and what doesn't in a low pressure environment. View it like a lab. If a routine doesn't work, then you may have to junk it. If parts of it don't work, then you'll know what to get rid of before going "live." If you're brave, you can practice in public in anonymous environments, but avoid going to your usual haunts until you've at least mastered some of the material.

After some practicing and adapting, the routine should become natural. This word "natural" is key. If your routines don't flow and aren't authentic, then you'll come across as a bad amateur stand-up comedian. It's better to use moderately funny original material than to have proven routines for other people fail because you can't deliver them authentically. This is also why practice in low pressure environments is important.

A popular person is always crafting, learning, and perfecting new routines. This ensures that you always have a huge archive of material from which to draw. If you see someone two days in a row, you don't want to repeat the same stuff or have nothing to say! Going from the life of the party to shy because you lack material makes you look like a faker or a one hit wonder.

Your routines should also be adaptable to every situation. In many cases, it's just a matter of shifting a few details or mentally picking the right routine at the right time. This is important to remember because, as I mentioned in the last chapter, situational humor is more personal, which means you'll get the best laughs and be the most memorable. For example, have a routine (or routines) that can be adapted for the high society party, the concert at the dive bar, and every environment in between.

Also, routines should never be a crutch to avoid coming up with original material on the fly. A celebrity is almost always popular because he's original. Copy cats are never as beloved as the people they're copying. People love the Beatles. They don't care about the guy who sings "Let It Be" down at the local Karaoke bar. So, be funny and original with your routines. This becomes easier the more you practice.

If you are stuck and can't think of a topic for original routines, think about funny stories or memorable events from your life. Then adapt them to situations. Perhaps you can use a routine about getting lost when you went camping when you were twelve. Maybe you can base one around an interesting story you heard from someone else. Just make sure your content is funny, authentic, and able to be adapted to any situation.

Keep in mind when writing routines that the stories about yourself should never make you look low value or creepy. If your routines involve some personal foible or funny incident, make sure they are cute and lighthearted. For example, telling a story about that snipe hunt your brother took you on when you were five is funny and cute. Telling a story about how a con man took your money when you were thirty just makes you look dumb. See the difference? Funny personal stories should always reinforce your positive traits or at least be neutral. They should never bring down your value in anyone's eyes.

To complete this chapter, write out at least two routines and practice them. I want these to be completely original! Make sure to throw in plenty of incongruity and observational humor, but don't violate the rule of safety. Include a short shaggy down story or an example of anti-humor into one of them. The point is to practice writing routines, not to write stand up worthy material right now.

Next chance you get, I want you to practice what you've just written with someone you trust. These are your stories, so they should be natural and authentic. However, in high stress environments like meeting strangers you may not be able to deliver your routines with ease. So, have your friend or family member give you feedback, not only on the material itself, but also on your delivery, timing, and so on. Humor will probably be the most important weapon you have to influence and win over others. Don't take it lightly!

CHAPTER 15

DETACH!

Awhile back, a friend told me about an open adjunct professor position at a local university. Since I still enjoyed teaching, I decided to apply for the fun of it. I didn't care if I even got the job since the position was a long drive and didn't pay a lot. It was a long, drawn out hiring process and, at each point where they cut candidates, I didn't expect to get any further. But, each time I moved on. Eventually, after almost seven months, they offered me the job. I'm convinced that I got the job over the other applicants simply because I didn't need it! Because I wasn't anxious, I was able to relax and show the committee my best self.

This story illustrates the importance of detachment. The opposite of attachment, detachment is thinking and acting in the best way possible, while not being concerned about a particular outcome. An outcome could be a job, friendship, money, or anything that we desire. The problem with being "attached" to an outcome is that often the strong emotions of attachment cloud our decisions.

Watch a show like American Idol sometimes. In the later rounds, the contestants are all great singers, the cream of the crop. However, many of them want to win so badly, they sometimes blow it by singing off key or choking in key moments. Their minds are clouded with feelings of attachment and it takes a toll. This is why detachment is considered a sign of enlightenment in many of the world's religions. We are at our best in all ways when we are detached.

You probably have many examples from your life of failing when you were attached, yet succeeding when you just simply decided you didn't care. On one episode of the 1980s sitcom "The Wonder Years," the teenage Kevin Arnold walks into baseball practice and, even though he isn't on the team, hits a home run. The coaches eagerly put him on the team, yet he struggles. Eventually he gets cut, but guess what happens when he steps up to the plate for one last swing? He hits a home run! That's detachment at work. A real world example almost everyone knows is the couple who tries to have kids, but can't. When they end up adopting, you know what comes next. They conceive.

Now, I'm not going to try to figure out the mind of God or the more mysterious laws of Universe, but for whatever reason, good things happen when we detach, but when we're desperately attached, we don't get our way. Perhaps detachment aligns us with the will of God or puts in harmony with the energy of the Universe. Or, maybe on a more earthly level, it's likely that we are our best, relaxed selves when we simply do our best and don't give a crap about what comes next. Detachment is a general success principle, but it's also vitally important for a celebrity in training. Why? Because a truly popular person will always be one of the most detached people in any environment.

In their endeavors, most people ignore the "process" of achieving a goal because they are too focused on the outcome. They wander through life, mindlessly going from goal post to goal post, never enjoying or appreciating what happens in between. Yet, a popular person knows the best things in life are found between the posts. In fact, that is where most of life happens. It's also where you meet and impress the people who will take you towards your ultimate goal of being popular and famous.

Let's take an example of a well-known celebrity like Brad Pitt. The guy can date any woman he wants, is set for life financially, and has his fill of fame. What outcome does he have to be attached to? None! He can go through life totally in the moment and let his true self shine through. He has to impress no one. I don't know Brad Pitt personally, so I'm not saying he lives a detached life, but he certainly could.

As you practice being popular with these techniques, detachment will be a key component of your success. You'll be approaching random people, getting their phone numbers, using new forms of humor, making bold and independent moves, and even experiencing setbacks on many occasions. These are not easy tasks. In fact, just mentioning them may be making you a little nauseous! That's all normal. But, it means you'll have to detach. You will have to make "it doesn't matter" your mantra when doing the difficult tasks this book recommends. If the professor shoots you down in class? It doesn't matter. Your humor falls flat in a group of strangers? It doesn't matter. You trip and fall in front of the popular girls at the student center? It doesn't matter.

However, don't think that being incredibly laid back and unmotivated is the same as detachment. People who are lazy aren't attached to any outcome because they don't pursue any valuable outcomes to begin with. They are simply adrift in life and often mooching off others (or settling in life). You can have passion, energy, and enthusiasm for your goals and still be detached from their outcomes.

Detachment, as I mentioned earlier, is considered an advanced spiritual technique and is regarded as a sign of enlightenment. Nonetheless, I'm going to attempt to give a small primer on how to achieve some form of detachment. It may not be enough to become a saint or the fifteenth Dalai Lama, but it will get you on your way to becoming more popular and, I truly believe, a better human being.

First, put everything in perspective. Remember the importance of perspective? That hasn't decreased in importance since the second chapter! The right perspective from a detachment standpoint is this: you can recover from anything short of death. So, the "it doesn't matter" mantra, if you're not six feet under, is always true. Life is a gift and as long as your heart is beating you have a second chance.

Let's examine my earlier examples. Your professor shoots your idea down. Is it really that big of a deal in the grand scheme of things? I can barely remember the names of all my professors, let alone individual incidents! Your humor falls flat among strangers. In a minute, they'll have forgotten about you, and by forty minutes, the scene will be fuzzy even in your mind. The popular girls see you fall. Who cares? After you put this book into practice, girls like them (maybe even them!) will be begging you for dates.

Second, practice mindfulness. A Buddhist concept, mindfulness is about paying attention in the present. You aren't oppressed by your past or apprehensive about the future. Your destination may be important, but the journey is just as important, if not more important. You take in the smells, the sounds, the sights, and above all, the feeling of your surroundings. You pay attention (see Chapter 25).

The value of mindfulness can be seen just by focusing on the world around you. To practice it right now, stop what you are doing and just non-judgmentally be aware of your breathing for a few moments. Pay attention to the feeling of the breath entering your nostrils and leaving your mouth. Believe it or not, something as simple as this is a powerful tool to help you relax and become more focused in the present.

Look at all the people who constantly dwell on the past. Their present is held hostage by events that ended long ago. Old memories and events emotionally cripple them in the present. The same is true, however, of those who worry about the future. Their stress about house payments, keeping down a job, and any number of "what if" scenarios makes the present miserable as they constantly worry about what possibly, maybe, might happen. I'm sure you know many people like this. In fact, it may even describe you! If so, you must let go and enjoy the present.

Practicing mindfulness regularly has the added benefit of creating deeper relationships with the people you encounter. You are genuinely paying attention to them instead of wishing they'd just be done talking already so you can worry about your credit card bill that's coming due or dwell a little longer on your bad relationship with your father. We humans can be so silly!

Think of the route you take to work, the signs, the background scenery, the details on the traffic lights, the shape of the trees, etc. Can you tell me about them? You're too focused on the road, you say, because you value safety? OK, tell me about the road then. Where does it twist and turn? Are the center lines yellow or white? Is there a curb? Tell me about the driveways that break up the road. If you don't know many details about the voyage you take five days a week, don't feel too bad. You're not all that different from most people. After all, your morning goal is to get to work, not take in the scenery.

If you want to be happy, successful, and popular, you must make mindfulness a priority. Make your choices based on a mindfulness mentality at all times. If you find yourself moving too quickly and becoming too focused on an outcome, take a step back and enjoy the little moments of life. If in doubt, just stop and take in everything your senses can handle. Smell. See. Taste. Touch. Listen. Notice how life slows down and your anxiety disappears. See how beautiful the world is. Just take a few deep breaths.

Third, detachment requires flexibility (see Chapter 7). There are many, many ways to get to an outcome. Just because you have one in your head doesn't make it the correct or even preferred method of achieving a goal. If a path towards your outcome doesn't seem to be working due to your own fault or an outside circumstance, then take another. The road to success often takes unique and surprising turns for many people. Don't give up on your dreams, but be flexible on the many trails that could take you there. Even supposed setbacks could be blessings in disguise, if you're flexible enough to adapt and can learn to grow from them.

Finally, to detach, you must devote some daily time to meditation. I'm not trying to convert you to any religion, just asking you to give a few minutes a day to relax, be mindful, and experience some quietude. If you're like most people, you could use some relaxation! Find a silent space, add some candles or other sensory aids, and just take it easy. Begin with several deep breaths. Be mindfully aware of the breathing in and breathing out. Once you're centered, you can just sit and reflect, pray, or even say your affirmations.

Whatever method you choose, the most important point of

meditation is to give yourself some quality time each day. I've never once wished I had spent my meditation time doing something else. Each and every time I've meditated, even if it was for five minutes, I've felt mentally more powerful and less stressed the entire day. So, even if you're extremely busy, make meditation a priority. Five minutes of meditation a day will make the remaining twenty-three hours and fifty-five minutes much more meaningful.

Tonight, I want you to take five minutes and meditate before bed. When you wake up tomorrow, do it again. If you can meditate longer, then keep going until you either want to stop or your schedule demands it. If you're not alone in your household, let everyone know that you are not to be bothered, except for emergencies. Turn off your cell phone and cover each visible clock. If you're using a meditation app on a computer or smart phone, then resist the urge to check other information like email. If you need to stop at a certain time, set an alarm, but otherwise, just go with the flow. This time is for you.

I know you may be laughing and thinking, "Why all the effort? It's only five minutes!" Can you stay focused and mindful for five whole minutes? In the age of text messages and the internet, don't be so sure! I have been meditating for several years now and I still have focus problems. You may be a natural meditator, but for the rest of us, I advise starting small and removing all distractions.

And, tomorrow I want you to focus on living in the present moment all day. Forget about yesterday and tomorrow and live for today. See how it affects you and others around you. It's very easy to

JONATHAN AND DAVID BENNETT

get into a pattern of mindless worry and stress, so you will probably have to be mindful of being mindful. Don't stress out, however. This exercise is supposed to make you less stressed and more detached. If you're having trouble, just return to mindful breathing and let your senses overtake you. Trust me, there is more than enough beauty in the present to keep you very busy for a long time if you train your brain to focus on it.

These tips may not seem intuitively designed to make you popular. However, don't neglect chapters that only seem remotely connected to being popular. They are some of the most important for your dream of fame, no matter how large or small, because they build a mentally powerful foundation upon which you will construct the new, popular, you.

This is a deep topic, so for more information, please visit the "Recommended Reading" section at the end of the book.

CHAPTER 16

BE POPULAR EVERYWHERE

In college, I had a great friend whom I'll call "Tony." A little older than most of the other students, he was funny, flexible, and charming, at ease with both professors and fellow students. Going out with him was always a blast. "Going in" with him, however, was a little different. One spring day, he invited my friends and me to his home to meet his wife. When we arrived, he was clearly nervous. While there, he was irritable, not nearly as friendly, and the guy who would stay out as long as he felt like it, asked us to leave the second the clock turned nine. We thought maybe he was upset with us, but the next time we went out, Tony was his usual fun and charming self.

I can't tell you why Tony acted this way at home. Perhaps his wife was uptight or he felt that he could only be himself with younger people or outside of the home. Regardless of his motives, Tony illustrates an important point: not only do we act differently in different environments, but we can be socially successful in some and utterly fail in others. After all, if we had first met Tony in his home, we'd probably never had wanted to see him again. In class and out on the town, however, it was a totally different story.

You've probably seen this phenomenon in action. You may have a co-worker who is great after hours, but becomes, during work, humorless and brash. Or perhaps your single best friend is great with the guys, but gets anxious around women. This behavior occurs because our brains become conditioned to behave differently as the environment changes. This makes a lot of sense from an evolutionary standpoint. For example, a guy who was loud and funny in his village was safe; if he tried those antics on a hunting trip he may have scared away dinner or become dinner himself. We've learned to act differently depending on the environment.

Think about the different environments you are in each day. If you're like the average person, they're probably work, home (or school), and your social life, although you may have others, as well as subsets of certain ones. How would you describe yourself in each setting? Flexible or rigid? Detached or attached? In charge or subservient? Do you exhibit your best qualities in each environment or only in a couple?

For most people, they will be closer to their best self in one environment and farther in others. Following the tips in this book will give you the tools necessary to succeed in any environment. However, there are ways to become instantly more popular and famous in whatever environment you find yourself.

First, typically, we act our best in environments where we are in charge. It's why most men with happy marriages and families are often confident at home since they can be themselves there. Their family won't fire them or demote them (well, not likely), but at work they may feel like they have to suppress their true feelings to kiss the boss's butt. This is also true for the person who never gets noticed in social settings. He can only watch with jealousy or fear as other, more outgoing people, take charge of the social hierarchy. So, to be popular anywhere you go, find a way to be in charge or at the top of the pecking order. It can be as short term as finding and befriending the hottest girl in a club or as long term as getting the training to be a manager at work.

Second, the most popular person in any environment is usually the one who is the most relaxed and flexible, especially in the face of stress. These are the people whom others want to befriend and lean on because they provide stability and relief in negative situations. If you work, live, or attend school in a negative place, then you make sure you stay out of the drama and be flexible enough to handle any predicament. Be the cool, charming person who can laugh off troubles while still maintaining his composure and you will be popular and excellent in every environment, even the low energy ones.

So, that means a true celebrity can, if he wants it, be popular wherever he finds himself. You have to start to internalize this mentality. While some environments may present more of a challenge, as long as there are humans present, they all operate according to human nature. That means whether it's a stuffy office where you work or a home dominated by an uptight wife, you will have the skills (when you're done with this book) to be a celebrity anywhere.

If you can be popular, loved, and well-known in every environment, then you will find that becoming popular is a breeze. Keep in mind that being famous (even locally) is really about making connections and winning fans. Recording a popular album or being in a hit movie is the fast way. But, if you become popular and loved everywhere you find yourself every single day, you will be a celebrity too. It's the slow lane, but it works, especially for those without a huge talent.

You're probably thinking a few things right now. Maybe your first thought about being a celebrity at work was "hell yeah." More likely you were thinking "Yeah right. Not with my co-workers." If you were imagining trying to be popular at the bars and clubs, maybe the nauseous feeling suddenly returned. These are old patterns and they will rear their ugly heads at the worst times. I urge you to not give up so easily. In fact, you can take your first step today and continue to cultivate your new, popular mindset. Don't let any place or environment scare you. You can be the master of them all.

For your practice assignment, I want you to refer back to your affirmations and declarations and the avatar you created based on them. Take every environment that you're in right now and write down how you can transform either yourself or the environment so that you're popular there. Remember that this typically involves becoming in charge of each setting. So, you should really be thinking about how to get more autonomy in your environments. For example, if you decide that you need to get a new job, then write down the concrete steps to get that job. Write "get a Monster.com account" and "send out two resumes a day," etc.

When you've finished your list for each of your environments, do something to get the process of transformation started right now. I mean it. If you're starting your own business, get on the Secretary of State's website and find out how to start an LLC after you've finished reading this chapter. If you want to talk to a beautiful girl at a coffee shop every night, go out tonight and talk to her! And don't go to bed until you've actually talked to someone!

And, remember that the more you become popular in every environment, the more you are expanding your fan base to become even bigger and more popular. Eventually, you want to be the person who's famous and beloved everywhere his feet touch the ground.

CHAPTER 17

BE VALUABLE TO OTHERS

Sometimes when I'm bored I'll engage in a little bit of inconspicuous people watching. I'm not creepy; I promise you. I do this because, as someone who helps others become their best, I think it's extremely important to be a student of human nature. And, watching it in the lab of life can be fascinating.

One day, while I was having coffee, I watched a very young, smart looking businessman walk in the coffee shop. He had on a nice pair of jeans and a button down shirt with no tie. I could see the female employees giggling as they debated over who would have the honor of serving him. He smiled at them and made eye contact. He was clearly relaxed in their presence and made a few jokes. He said he didn't have much time because of a business deal, but he enjoyed their brief acquaintance. As he left, I heard them talking about his fifty percent tip. One of them said, "Gosh, why can't I have a boyfriend like him?!"

Look at the information this man gave me (and the people in the coffee shop). Dressed in a trendy, yet professional manner. Working on projects for his own business. Ease with strangers. Personally funny with a good sense of humor. Polite. Generous. Good looking enough to warrant the attention of people working there. Although I didn't know this man personally, I wish I did!

A few minutes later, another notable customer walked through the door. He was overweight, had his shirt slightly un-tucked, and had sweat under his armpits. He told the cashier he was in a hurry because he was late to work. When she smiled and asked him what he did, he looked down, frowned and said, "Oh, just some dumb office job." She accidentally gave him the wrong flavor shot in his coffee and he became impatient with her. He didn't leave a tip and loudly proclaimed for all to hear that the tip jar was pointless with such bad employees. After he walked out the door, one employee told the other: "Sheesh, that guy was a huge jerk."

Now, let's review the information this man gave me. Nervous. Not so good looking and unconcerned with looking his best. Has a bad job or at least a bad attitude towards his job. Impatient and unforgiving. Stingy and condescending. Like the first specimen, I didn't know this man personally. If I had my way, I would never, ever want to befriend this guy or even work alongside him.

Who do you think appeared "high value" that day? In other words, who appeared as a person who would be worth knowing? Who appeared "low value," meaning not worth knowing? Although you may have different tastes, most people would rather know a relaxed, generous good looking business owner than a gruff, sweaty cog in the machine who treats others with contempt.

One of the biggest keys to being popular is to project your high value to the world. All genuine celebrities have a high value or worth in the eyes of others. They are valuable for their power, their money, their ability to entertain, even their looks. Yes, some people have value because others like to stare at them. Value and worth are interconnected. Whatever the reason, a celebrity is worth knowing and loving. Unpopular people are generally not worth knowing because they typically offer little in the way of value to the world. Either that or they are poor at communicating their worth to others.

Right now you may be doubting your value. You may not be much to look at and maybe you don't have a lot of money. And, if you're like the vast majority of Americans, you don't own a business or run the show at work. On your bad days, you may not treat people very well either. Are you low value or high value? Maybe you're somewhere in between, which can happen sometimes. Give an honest answer! Also, make sure that what you have to offer is something the world values. The people of the world value individuals who can meet their needs; they don't really care that you've reached the highest level of experience points in the latest Final Fantasy installment or that your virtual pumpkins on a Facebook game are ready to pick (even if those took you a lot of time and effort).

If you think you're high value (ask an unbiased observer just to be sure), then your goal is simply to project it more often (Chapter 22). If you've determined you're low value, then you have to raise your value. The good news is that value is relative and, while money, power, good looks, and being well-connected can help, certain traits also project value and they are absolutely free! And, incidentally, those traits can lead to money and power down the line if you use them to become nationally or world famous. Now, I'm going to list a few specific examples of ways to raise your value cheaply. You'll find that many of these tips are discussed in more details in other chapters of this book.

First, humor is a great way to demonstrate your high value. Truly witty people are a rarity in this world which is why good comedians are well-compensated. If something is rare, then people assign it more value. In addition, by making others laugh, you are relieving stress and making them feel better. This ability is highly valued (see the money spent on depression meds and psychologists). So, be funny, share it with others and they will consider you valuable (see Chapter 13).

Second, extroversion is a high value trait. How many new people talk to you on a daily basis? One? Two? Sometimes most of us may go a whole week or more and not have anyone new, outside of a salesperson, talk to us. Striking up a conversation with new people and building rapport with them show that you are a confident, high value person because so many people are lonely and have no one to interact with them in a meaningful way.

Third, taking charge of situations shows you are high value. If you can't move up the ladder at work or start your own business just yet, then figure out a way to be in charge of anything. Coordinate volunteers for a charity event or start your own club or group. Create a company newsletter. Become the president of a church committee. Organize a park cleanup. Do anything that puts you in charge. It's an added bonus if your leadership opportunity interests a lot of people because then you can be in charge of large numbers and use them for networking.

Another tip to be high value is to simply avoid doing things perceived as being low value. That's right, sometimes by not making too many mistakes, you can fake it. Some examples of low value behavior are: arrogance, whining, playing the victim, timidity, being uptight, rigid and/or controlling, outbursts of anger, lacking composure in stressful situations, being a tattle tale, gossiping, etc. Avoid these and anything else you may think will make you look less valuable in the eyes of others.

The best way to act with high value on a daily basis is to ask yourself a simple question: "If I saw someone else acting this way, would I consider that person worth knowing?" If your tastes are eclectic, then replace "I" with "the average person." In most cases you should be able to figure it out. For example, throwing a hissy fit with your girlfriend in public isn't high value in anyone's book. In addition, you should find people you admire (like the man in the first paragraph) and act like them.

Right now, I'd like you to list ways in which you are talented and high value. If you're not high value enough, which is probably the case since we can all become more valuable, then write down traits you can cultivate and actions you can take to become more worth knowing. Re-examine your affirmations and declarations to see examples of traits that will help you become your best self and reach your goals.

CHAPTER 18

ASSERT YOURSELF!

When I was a teacher, an administrator started attending our departmental meetings with increased regularity. It was unusual because this wasn't standard practice. Not only that, but she constantly interrupted our discussions, even shooting down our ideas. Most of us were too afraid to say anything for fear of losing our jobs – except for one person: Adam. He asked her, respectfully, what she was doing at our meetings and told her, also with respect, that he didn't like her constantly micromanaging our affairs. She didn't really answer him, but said nothing the rest of the meeting. In fact, after that she didn't even attend another one.

Adam was our hero. He said what everyone else had been

thinking, even though we didn't have the guts to vocalize it. If you look at the people who are beloved throughout history, nearly all of them asserted themselves in some way. Great figures like Joan of Arc, Martin Luther King, Jr., Gandhi, and others won praise and admiration because they had the courage to assert themselves, usually in a firm, but non-violent way. The people who remained silent? The vast majority of them are lost to history.

The reason society values assertive people is because most people admire the qualities of confidence and leadership. Men and women who can assert themselves in appropriate ways are valued and respected and attain what all people seeking celebrity ultimately want: fans. However, being assertive is an art and it's very difficult for some people, especially shyer ones.

There are a variety of reasons why individuals (including perhaps yourself as you read this) do not assert themselves more often. First, a lot of people think that being assertive is the same as being mean. So, they don't speak up for fear of offending other people. Second, there are those who fear asserting themselves because they fear the consequences.

Being assertive in an environment where a person is not in charge can sometimes result in consequences from a "superior." We've been taught since we were in school to obey our alleged betters. Consequently, many of us have an irrational fear of speaking our minds unless we're the boss (and even then it can be tough).

I also want to briefly touch on what I call "nice guy syndrome." This often afflicts men who, in the name of being nice and kind, never stand up for themselves and go with the flow to the point of being taken advantage of. They smile through everything, never stand up to anybody, even when it's just, and think that being nice will result in life handing them every advantage.

Well, the phrase "nice guys finish last" is popular for a reason. Women dislike nice guys. Nice guys get pushed around at work. Their friends and strangers don't respect them. Oh, and deep down, they're not even really "nice." They're frustrated by their situation and many of them explode on their families or friends and eventually have nervous breakdowns. If you are a nice guy, then that has to end. You can be a good guy, an excellent guy, but as of today, it's "no more Mr. Nice Guy."

If you want to be assertive, you'll not only have to stop being passive, but you'll also have to avoid the other extreme on the spectrum: aggression. Sadly, a lot of leaders move beyond being assertive to being violent. It doesn't even have to be physical violence.

I've known many teachers, bosses, and institutional leaders who've done emotional, mental, and other types of damage just with their words or actions. Basically, when you stand up for your opinion, if it is done in a way that harms others, then you've passed into aggression. This can include putting others down, using sarcasm, yelling, bullying, violating personal space, making threats, etc. Aggression isn't just jerk behavior; it's also ineffective in the long term. Aggressive people may get their way in the short term, but over time their actions can destroy organizations, erode their personal popularity, and drastically limit their number of genuine followers. Aggressive people have toadies, not fans.

You'll also want to avoid another type of behavior: being passive-aggressive. This is essentially being aggressive, but doing it in an indirect, passive way. For example, let's say someone takes your coleslaw from the fridge at work. An aggressive response would be to yell at the person who took it and threaten him. A passive-aggressive response would be to announce at the lunch table for all to hear that there are worthless thieves who steal people's food. A more extreme example would be stealing from someone else as "retaliation."

As a preview, an assertive person would respectfully tell the offender not to take your lunch next time. With passive-aggressive behavior, the aggressive intent is still obvious. However, being passive-aggressive is considered very low value. It makes a person (especially a man) look weak because he can't directly deal with his problems. If you are passive-aggressive, cut it out right now.

Now, it's time to move on to the good stuff: being assertive. Here are my most helpful techniques to assert yourself whenever necessary and appear like a high value, confident man (or woman).

First, always make sure you're relaxed and detached. Being afraid (even of consequences), enraged, stressed, or emotional when asserting yourself will hinder your success. You have to be seen as cool and relaxed. In the example of my colleague, he was matter of fact when he confronted his boss. She didn't sense any fear or aggression. You don't want others to sense that in you either. If they think you're operating from fear, anger, or any other negative emotion they'll likely ignore you or dismiss you in some fashion.

Second, avoid the language and action of judgment. This is much easier when you're detached and relaxed, I might add. When you assert yourself in any situation, this is extremely important. Stick to the facts and your own opinions and needs without belittling or judging others. In fact, it's best to avoid "you" statements altogether because saying "you" frequently in a conversation with other people comes across as judgmental, especially in more stressful conversations. A few paragraphs down I've given some examples of how to speak without judgment.

Third, try to empathize with the other people involved. Empathy is the ability to understand others and to try to share their feelings. Showing empathy is related to not judging others. While people make boneheaded decisions, in most cases when you need to assert yourself, the individuals in question aren't trying to be evil or purposefully nasty. It's helpful to try to understand the motivation behind the person's behavior and then express that empathy when you assert yourself. You can often say, "I understand that..." to begin your conversation. This is where you acknowledge the person's feelings, so they don't think you're attacking them.

Fourth, when you assert yourself, try to offer the person an olive branch, especially if you're disagreeing with him or her about something. Human nature dictates that when we feel like we're "losing" we tend to dig in our heels and get defensive. Yet, if we feel like we're being understood and getting something out of a deal, we're more likely to get on board. So, when you stand up to someone or have to be assertive, offer something in the way of compromise. Below are a few examples of how to be assertive with empathy, non-judgment, and compromise.

Scenario - Your roommate is playing music at night, keeping you awake

Wrong response - "You are an inconsiderate idiot! Don't you know I work the morning shift?"

Right response - "I understand that music relaxes you at night, but I need my sleep for my morning shift. Could you please either use headphones or turn it down?"

Observations - Notice how the correct response focuses on the need for sleep and lacks name calling? Also, it shows an understanding of why the roommate plays music as well as a suggestion that both parties can embrace.

<u>Scenario</u> - Your boss has been disrespectful towards you

Wrong response - "You have been such a jerk towards me lately. You need to lay off or I'm going to your manager."

Right response - "I know you've been under a lot of stress lately, with the new merger and all. However, I've really felt frustrated lately because I have a need to be respected. Since you're very professional, I know it must've been inadvertent. If you need help with your workload, I'd be happy to contribute in any way I can."

Observation - Notice how the second response reserves judgment? There's no language of being a jerk and it recognizes that stress played a role and it had to be inadvertent (even if it wasn't). It also subtly praises the boss (calling her professional). It also extends an olive branch, by offering to help with the work load. While the boss is unlikely to take the help, just receiving an offer would likely engender feelings of gratitude.

Another part of being assertive is learning to say "no." For whatever reason, a lot of people have a hard time doing this. It could be a desire to please others or maybe fear that saying no could result in a loss of a job, opportunity, or a friendship. However, not being able to say "no" often causes great stress since it creates overbooking and can lead to resentment. If we don't want to be doing something, our work on it typically isn't the best either.

Like learning how to assert yourself, saying "no" is also an art. While the previous tips are valuable for saying "no," here is some specific advice.

The first thing to remember when saying "no" is to remember the reason why you're being asked to do something. In most cases, you are being asked because you are good at what you do or because the person asking has a real need. When I worked a summer job at Kmart, I used to get upset when I would be called about taking extra hours. However, now I realize I received calls because I was a good employee and the manager needed coverage for the store to function properly. I still would've said "no" in many cases, but my perspective certainly would've been better.

Second, when you say "no" do it with non-judgment, empathy, and compromise. Typically, it's helpful to thank the person for thinking of you. Then, if possible, offer some kind of way to help them meet their needs or to put them in contact with someone who can. If you tell people "no" in ways that are snarky or negative, they won't want to follow you or be around you much. In case it's still unclear, below I've given a few examples of how to say "no" properly.

Scenario - Your boss needs you to work on a project, but you're swamped

Wrong response - "I can't do that! Don't you know I'm totally swamped?"

Right response - "Thanks for thinking of me for this, but I just have no time this week. Once I finish this project, I'd be happy to help another team member with it."

Observation - The first response is defensive and gives no compromise. The second one, however, shows gratitude for the offer and then a willingness to do it: at a later time and with some help. Both of those are reasonable requests a boss will likely allow, so long as there isn't a vital time deadline.

Scenario - A friend asks to borrow fifty dollars for a concert

Wrong response - "No"

Right response - "I understand you're going through a rough patch and really love that band, but I don't have fifty dollars to lend [or I would]."

Observation - The first response is wrong because it's abrupt and doesn't take the other person's feelings into account. Borrowing money for a concert may seem dumb, but if the person asking loves the artist in question, he probably doesn't think of it that way. So, by being understanding and honest about your financial situation, you are showing empathy and setting yourself up for some in return. I added "or I would" in brackets because with favors and money requests, you always have to weigh them carefully. If this person is unreliable, then you don't want to promise him money at a later date. However, if he is reliable, then you can.

So, try to be more assertive in your life and do so in all environments. If people know you as a passive person, they may be shocked at first. But, if you assert yourself in ways that are respectful using the tips outlined in this chapter, then they will ultimately value you and respect you more. For practice, I'd like you to write down five ways in which you'd like to assert yourself. Make them specific. You likely know in what areas you'd like to do this. It could be as mundane as to assert yourself when a restaurant messes up your order to as large as demanding that your wife stop cheating on you. Whatever you pick, next write out an action plan that is empathetic, non-judgmental, and shows some compromise. Resolve to carry out your new assertive goals as soon as possible!

CHAPTER 19

LOOKS DON'T MATTER (AS MUCH AS YOU THINK)

When I was in college, I was in a club with some friends and we met a guy who claimed to be a pickup artist. We just laughed. He was clearly at least one hundred pounds overweight and was balding. He smiled and told us to watch. He went up to a group of girls and used a few of his techniques. Within seconds they were laughing and hanging on his every word. We lost contact with this guy until he left the bar an hour or so later. Sure enough, as he walked out the door, he had a young lady holding onto his arm. I just wished I had asked for some of his tips instead of just laughing him off.

As I became more and more popular myself, I had to unlearn this deeply ingrained lesson about looks. The truth, at least for men, is that they simply don't matter all that much. And, for women who have the goal of general popularity and not sex appeal, the same is true. I say this as someone who works out six days a week, always eats right, and generally takes care of himself. But, the facts are facts.

Even so, you may be snickering as a slideshow of handsome Hollywood stars runs through your head. While it's true the majority are good looking, nonetheless it isn't essential to becoming famous. Let me give you a few names: Danny DeVito, Rosie O'Donnell, Roseanne Barr, Steve Buscemi, Clint Howard, etc. Now, I'm not putting any of these people down. Even if I did laugh at them, why should they care about my opinion? They're laughing all the way to the bank (in addition to the fame and the other perks of being a celebrity) and some of it is from my money!

My primary point is that looks don't really matter as much as you think when it comes to being popular. Sure, it may have seemed that way in high school and maybe college, but I'm confident you can think of exceptions even in those settings. As a result of the "looks are essential" myth, countless people who don't live up to Hollywood's impossible standards (photo-shopping anyone?) think they are doomed to a life of obscurity. Nothing could be further from the truth. Celebrities are made, not born, remember (see Chapter 1)?

But, a popular person still needs to look his best. That's right. Looks won't stop you from being popular and a success, but studies and experience show that being pretty or handsome is an asset, whether it's at work or at home. And, it's another weapon that you should have in your arsenal of becoming a celebrity. Basically, if you are mentally, intellectually, and emotionally excellent (which is what this book is essentially trying to help you be), then you should be physically excellent as well. And, the more of these assets you have in your favor, the easier being popular and famous becomes.

When I say you should try to have good looks, don't fret. I'm not talking about Megan Fox or Robert Pattinson level of hotness. Basically, I just want you to look your best in public at all times. That is what you see of almost all celebrities, even if they look their best according to their "image," which may be sloppy and unkempt. It takes a lot of work for some of those guys to make their hair look like they just woke up!

Below are my general tips for looking your best. I'm not an expert by any means, but I do try to look my best all the time and regularly consult professionals in regard to dress, health, and other issues. If you have a particularly glaring need in the looks department, consult an expert in that field (like a hair stylist, weight loss consultant, etc.). But, these tips should at least help you make some minor adjustments and get you thinking about what it means to look your best.

Hygiene

Take regular showers and use deodorant. Especially make sure to wash areas that sweat a lot and your bodily orifices (enough about that topic). Bad smell is a huge turn off and you will repulse people. Use cologne or perfume, but don't overdo it. You won't win fans if they're having an allergic reaction to you!

Another huge issue is bad breath. Brush and floss each day, especially if you smoke or drink a lot of coffee (but you should quit smoking). Don't forget to brush the tongue and gum areas. That's where a lot of stench-inducing bacteria can hide. Make sure you wash your clothes too, since a smelly shirt will undo any benefits that come with a shower.

Take care of your feet too. This means washing them and even changing socks and shoes when they start to stink. Foot odor can be very nauseating.

A somewhat forgotten area of hygiene is the hands. Make sure you keep your hands looking nice. Don't bite your nails, regularly trim them, and keep your hands well moisturized. Cracked, dry skin can look very ugly and gross. It's especially important to keep your hands hydrated in the winter when dry skin is more prevalent.

Clothes

Your clothes should be trendy, but not so trendy that you're just a clone. For example, I have nothing against Ed Hardy shirts, but when everyone else is wearing an Ed Hardy shirt at a place, you'll just blend in. Same with brands like Aeropostale, Hollister, etc. Those just scream follower and a celebrity is a leader. You don't want to be outlandish, but be stylish in your own unique way.

Be realistic with your clothes types and sizes. If you're forty, look trendy for forty, not "forty going on sixteen." You'll just look like a forty year old trying desperately to look sixteen and be the laughingstock of both age groups. Also, if you're pudgy, skip the skinny jeans and the tight tops. Base your choices on who you are now, not who you were twenty years ago or who you want to be after you lose those ten pounds. Once you lose the weight, then go buy the new wardrobe.

Hair and Face

Make sure your haircut is trendy. For guys, never do a comb-over. If you're bald, just shave. Otherwise, you'll look like you're hiding something. Avoid facial hair too. Beards will make you look older, which is OK if you have a baby face; but otherwise avoid them. Unless you're a genuinely tough guy, avoid goatees. I've never met a girl yet who finds them attractive.

For the book's women readers, a trendy haircut is also a must since female styles tend to go out of fashion much more quickly than those of men. The worst you can do is look like you're from a different decade. Also, really short hair may be easier, but it is never preferable. If you want to be sexy, keep it at least shoulder length. Take it from a guy. As for your makeup, be trendy, but not gaudy. And if you cake on the makeup because you have something to hide, everyone else knows what you're doing. So, just be natural.

Make sure to cleanse and moisturize your face regularly. This goes for both men and women. This will help you prevent or heal the ravages of age. It will also help you avoid dry skin and pimples. Both of those have a high "gross out" factor, which could instantly turn off people as you meet them.

Height

For women, this advice is second nature. If you're really short you can wear heels; if you're really tall and don't want to appear too manly, wear flats. No biggie.

For men, the issue is different. Society tends to value tallness, but short of the platform shoe craze of the 70s, hasn't really provided short men with a socially acceptable way to mask their stature. If you're short, you have a couple options. The first is to do nothing. You don't have to be tall to be popular, even with women. I see short guys have success in this department all the time. However, I don't recommending wearing clothes that accentuate your shortness. This means you should avoid horizontal stripes, big patterns, and overly baggy outfits.

The second option is to enhance your height in some way. You can do this by purchasing shoes with larger heels or even shoes with lifts. Insertable lifts are available too. If you increase your height by a couple of inches, make sure you can still walk! And avoid situations where you may be asked to remove your shoes. Society already thinks short people are insecure and the last thing you want to do is confirm that impression. It should also be noted that many people, especially women, are particularly observant. So, if you gain three inches in a day, you may have to explain yourself.

Weight

I've saved the most touchy issue for last. In the United States and many Western countries, obesity has become an epidemic. This has serious health implications, but is an aesthetic issue as well. Ironically, the ideal man and woman in the media are getting thinner while real men and women are getting fatter.

Being fat won't stop you from being a celebrity, it's true. Look at John Candy, Dom Delouise and many others. However, the truth is most people will find you more attractive if you are skinny, but not too skinny. The ideal look could be described as generally "fit." For men, that means not overdoing it on the extreme muscle gain either.

Not only will you find popularity becomes easier, but losing weight has other advantages as well. You can fit into trendier clothing, won't sweat as much, and will probably have fewer health problems.

It's beyond the scope of this book to give you diet and exercise advice. However, I personally like Fitday (www.fitday.com) to keep track of calories, and Beachbody's Insanity series or P90x to get a great workout. Also, just simply walking for thirty to sixty minutes a day with friends will help you shed excess weight. This two pronged approach of cutting calories and working out will give you the most success in losing weight healthily and quickly. However, if you need to lose weight and/or get fit, you'll need to consult a doctor first.

Your assignment is to write down areas where you think you need to improve your looks. For each area you write down, come up with a few ways you can make yourself look better. They can be little things you can do now or possibly long term solutions that involve a professional. Try to be fairly specific, then start working to reach those goals immediately.

CHAPTER 20

CUT THE CREEPINESS

I knew a guy in college (not very well thankfully) who would draw images of violent pornography. He was a pretty good looking man who could actually be fairly charming at times. He made acquaintances easily. However, when he showed other people his drawings, most of those acquaintances didn't turn into close friends. This guy, like many people out there, was bona fide creepy. And, let me tell you, being creepy is a deal-breaker for most people when determining if they want to be your friend. If you're creepy, in spite of any other social assets you might have, your dreams of becoming more popular will be flushed down the toilet.

Being creepy means you create a feeling of uneasiness in others. It isn't just what you say that can be creepy. Your looks, mannerisms, body language, dress, gestures, etc. can also make other people feel ill at ease. Creepiness is sometimes in the eye of the beholder. However, in general, creepiness, for the vast majority of people, is a lot like how Supreme Court Justice Potter Stewart defined pornography: you know it when you see it.

Being creepy sends out a bad vibe. It says you are weird, have low value, and even worse, that you may be dangerous. As mentioned previously, you may have everything going for you, but being creepy will invalidate all your other advantages. Picking up on creepy behavior is likely an evolutionarily developed trait. That behavior tells our brains that the creepy person is not normal and we'd better be extra careful because he (most creepers are dudes) could be dangerous.

If you think you may be creepy, don't get the notion that you can master every technique in this book and become a celebrity. Someone who is creepy, but gains confidence, just becomes even more creepy – like a creep on steroids. A lady I know has a friend who is filthy rich and handsome, yet he's always single. He cries when he's drunk at parties because he feels guilty about having sex with call girls. In other words, he may be rich, but no female in her right mind wants to be around him.

If anything in this chapter sounds like you or you've been called creepy before, keep reading. It is absolutely essential that you lose the creepy vibe immediately. Since you may have been creepy your entire life, being non-creepy could require work, but like every other problem you face in this book, it's not impossible to change your behavior. The first step is to be self-aware. You must be able to understand your thoughts, actions, and how your thoughts influence your actions. I've written an entire chapter on this that should offer additional help (Chapter 25).

Second, get some feedback from friends and acquaintances and act on the feedback. Go out with some guys that you know are not creepy, and have them take a look at how you interact with people. If they see anything creepy, have them tell you. Some creepy behavior may be accidental, like an off-hand comment or gesture, but other things you do and say might be regular creepy occurrences, and it is important that you know it. You can also model these non-creepy friends. Watch their limits especially. The difference between charming and creepy hinges usually on what is *not* said. This is because while everyone has occasional abnormal thoughts and impulses, creepy people typically share those publicly and even act on them. You must learn to develop a filter.

Keep in mind a few topics that typically make most people uncomfortable: death, rape, violence, disabilities, sexual aggression, fetishes, etc. If it's rated NC17 or you have to be 21 to learn more about it on the internet, it's best to avoid it in conversation, especially when dealing with total strangers. Even with friends, you probably don't want to bring up your deviancy. Better still, stop being deviant!

Finally, change creepy behavior. If you're going to succeed you'll have to learn to self-censor and get rid of those old patterns. This will come over time, by taking control of your thoughts and constantly modeling other people for appropriateness. If you can't shake the creepy mentality, you'll possess a bunch of positive traits, but one seemingly small hindrance will invalidate them all. Your brain can be rewired and you'll have to get those non-creepy neurons firing.

If you fail the creepy test, your homework is to write out a plan to stop being creepy based on my tips in this chapter. If you aren't creepy, then congratulations. The world has one less oddball to deal with!

CHAPTER 21

BREAK FROM THE HERD

When I was in seventh grade the "big man on campus" was a guy by the name of Eric. He was witty, athletic, and cool. Naturally, I wanted to be like Eric. So, I started talking like him and acting like him, even imitating some of his goofy voices. To top it off, I actually started drawing my own "version" of a comic book character he created. After a few weeks of aping his behavior, a teacher sat me down and told me what everyone else was thinking. The school needed what Jonathan Bennett brought to the table; it already had one Eric.

What I went through was common. When we find someone who seems to have what we desire, such as popularity and success, we naturally want to model that person. And, modeling is a great way to improve ourselves. Yet, most of us go beyond modeling and adapting our own behavior (which is somewhat tough) to completely mimicking the other person (which is easy)! We want to look just like him, act just like him, and even do the same things he does. What we fail to realize is that most people are liked because they are unique, not because they blend in.

Breaking from the herd can be risky, but is often worth it!

However, blending in is the norm. And, for good reason. Humans are weak and puny compared to saber toothed tigers and wooly mammoths. We banded together into herds (which we call communities or tribes) because of the safety that comes with numbers.

By working together, early humans could also cooperate to achieve more than they ever could as individuals. This has led to civilization as we know it.

But, the herd isn't always the best place if you want to be noticed. Look at a bunch of zebras running on the African plains. Can you tell one from another? Probably not. But humans are nothing like that, right? Well, how about the number of white shirts and ties on the subway any weekday morning? If you still aren't convinced, go to a high school football game and count the number of Hollister, Aeropostale, or Abercrombie and Fitch shirts.

If you want to be popular, you must separate from the herd. In today's world, this simply means you must be original and forge your own path. However, doing your own thing can still be scary because you'll leave the safety of the group. You may not have to dodge lions and tigers, but you may be heckled, mocked, and outright ridiculed. But, if you're successful, the reward can be great.

In the early 1950s music had become boring and stale. "How Much Is That Doggie In the Window?" was a number one hit for *eight weeks* in 1953. This lame trend in music led several young musicians to rebel from the status quo, to break away and do their own thing. The result was rock and roll as we know it (7).

In the beginning, rock music was denounced as evil, anti-Christian, and a corrupter of youth. That's right. It seems silly now, but acts like Buddy Holly and Bill Haley were "of the devil!" Records were smashed, songs were banned, and musicians were denounced from church pulpits. However, the musical artists who started rock and roll broke from the herd and exposed themselves to the (metaphorical) lions. They blazed a new trail and found countless followers. There was a herd, but they formed it and were at the front of it. They became beloved celebrities and now are considered innovators and musical legends.

Your challenge is to stand out in your own way. After all, most people will encounter tens, if not hundreds, of people each day. In most cases everyone they meet is almost exactly the same in personality, style, and blandness. If people meet you, what makes you any different? If you're not unique in some way, you won't be a celebrity. The reason is simple: you're forgettable! Just like everyone else.

You're probably thinking I'm going to tell you to break from the herd by being yourself. Well, I'm not. Being yourself is horrible advice because most people absolutely hate themselves! My advice to be popular is to be your *best* self (see Chapter 6). Take the traits you outlined in your affirmations and assigned to your avatar and actually live them. Hopefully you put some big dreams in there. Go out and fulfill them and you will have no trouble breaking from the herd.

I hope it goes without saying that being a freak isn't the same as breaking from herd. Yes, being weird will probably get you out of the herd (kicked out!), but you won't get any followers. A serial killer is unique, but other than fellow twisted human beings, he's not going to have any fans. If you stand out from the crowd in a really creepy way, you will never be a celebrity, unless you are very talented and your freakishness is part of your act (like Marilyn Manson or Alice Cooper). In general, you must stand out by being original and excellent, not by being a creepy loser.

Your practice assignment is to list ten things that are unique about you. These are your interests, talents, style, etc. that separate you from the herd. Think about how the average person looks, acts, etc. and how you deviate from them (in a positive way, of course). Maybe you are happy at work while everyone else is grumpy. Maybe you can ride a unicycle. Whatever you identify as your unique traits, write them down.

Next, I want you to think about ways your unique self can shine through. Think about how you act at work, at school, in social settings, etc. Do you blend in? Do you take any risks? Chances are you conform for the sake of safety. I'd like you to try to break out of that routine a little bit. Don't do anything that will get you arrested, fired, suspended, or sent to the funny farm, but try to make your unique traits evident in environments where you normally act like everyone else.

Being your best self may be scary at first. It's natural to feel this way. However, remember you want to be popular, not just an average person. Gradually, you'll find it easier to let the best traits of your true self shine before everyone. I think you'll discover that people around you will begin to appreciate your independence and uniqueness.

However, if you find that your best self isn't welcome at work or with certain friends, then it's probably time to find places where you are more accepted and make some new, more supportive friends. At the school where I used to teach, conformity among staff was the norm. Creativity and fun were a definite no-no. Let's just say it wasn't an environment where I could thrive as a teacher, even though I was the most popular teacher there among students. Now, writing books and speaking, I'm in a much better place for my natural talents. Remember, as a celebrity you must create your own reality. Others don't create it for you.

CHAPTER 22

DON'T FEAR SELF PROMOTION

When I was in high school, I volunteered to be a student helper in a fourth grade classroom. It mainly consisted of grading papers and cutting out laminated sheets (ad nauseum!). However, one day I got to judge Valentine's Day shoe boxes that the children had designed. I shared this honorable duty with four of their parents who had agreed to help the teacher with the day's party.

I closely examined each shoe box, putting deep thought into picking the winners of each category. When I gathered with the four parents to justify my reasoning, I dutifully explained the method behind my choices. It turns out my efforts at impartiality were totally pointless. Each mother had chosen her child to win one of the awards!

It was hilarious to hear each woman's tortured argument as to why her son or daughter should win. Looking back, I think some of the mothers even volunteered for the sole purpose of making sure their kid won a stupid certificate that I'm sure has long since been thrown away.

I did, however, learn a valuable lesson that day. You must promote the hell out of yourself if you want to be successful. Because if you don't, no one else will, especially in the beginning. Those parents understood that if their children wanted to win any sort of award, someone had to be fighting for them. It sounds ridiculous and shady (I thought so when I encountered these four mothers), but it's also the way the world works.

Fortunately, I was taught the virtue of humility as a child. However, I overcompensated, foolishly believing that true talent would be recognized and no one should toot his or her own horn. Let me tell you from personal experience, that view is crappy! Most people are too busy pursuing their own interests to devote loads of time promoting your dream. That's why the advice I give everyone who will listen is this: promote yourself. If you have a business, tell everyone about it at every opportunity. If you have a talent, express it to anyone who's interested, and even those who may not be at first. The worst anyone can say is "no," and if you hear "yes," then the sky could be the limit.

Let me give you a tale of two of my former students. One was a good singer, but never practiced. She fantasized about making it big, but wouldn't even go out on a limb and sing at the school's chapel services. I guess she thought a record producer or agent would take one look at her and decide she was a top level talent without ever hearing her voice! On the other hand, there was another girl who sang all the time at school events, including the yearly talent show. She also entered every possible competition and even traveled to Los Angeles to create opportunities for fame and success. While no one is a sure thing to make it big, I do guarantee this: the girl who self-promoted and put one hundred percent of her effort into becoming a successful singer has a much greater chance of achieving her dreams than the one who never sang or promoted her talents.

You may be thinking it's arrogant to always be promoting yourself and your interests. It can be. However, there's a difference between bragging and demonstrating your talents. If you constantly talk about how awesome of a guitarist you are, but can't really play or never "put up," then you need to shut up. However, if you have an awesome talent, a great idea, or something else that is unique and valuable about you, then you'll have to share it and get it out in the world yourself. Imagine if the great innovators of the world just kept their ideas to themselves. Likely you wouldn't even be reading this book (certainly not on an electronic device).

I talk about my speaking and writing activities all the time and people love it. In fact, in almost every case, they like it so much they want to be a part of it in some way. So, by promoting myself, I get new contacts for my business and the people I meet may either need what I offer or be able to share in its success. In a former business venture of mine, my partner told a lady about our business and we discovered she was a graphic designer. She designed the layout for this book! Did I mention she was a Starbucks barista at the time? Yes, just being friendly with a random employee resulted in a graphic designer. And, her friendliness and willingness to promote herself got her a job!

Also, even if people may not be that interested in what you're doing, at least you're getting your name and your ideas out there. Maybe the person you talk to at McDonald's doesn't have a need for your talents. But, if you are friendly and promote yourself, perhaps she has a cousin or friend who does. And, if you've promoted yourself effectively, she'll probably let that person know about you. In addition, just having a talent or a good idea and sharing it sets you apart from most of the population that live in mediocrity their entire lives. It instantly makes you appear more high value (see Chapter 17).

I have a few helpful tips for you to promote yourself. The first is to never, ever lie about yourself and your talents. I knew a guy in elementary school who told a bunch of whoppers all the time, like how he was a bat boy for various major league baseball teams and launched a water rocket to the moon. We loved him for his wondrous deeds. Until we found out he was lying. Then, his value went way down in our eyes. You don't want to make a bunch of outrageous claims and then be called on them. You will quickly lose friends and popularity.

However, you must always put the best spin on what you do. You have to "set the frame" when promoting yourself, which means instead of letting someone get a bad or neutral impression of you, do your best to establish a positive impression. For example, a house that I think is a dump could easily be a "fixer upper" or a "starter home" if marketed correctly to the right people. Also, there's no need to disclose everything about yourself, especially your failures. You don't see major companies announcing their bankruptcies or other negatives on their television ads. If you're just starting out you can tell the truth and then shift the focus to your amazing potential.

Second, if you have a talent, a business, or a great idea, you'd better damn well be passionate and positive about it. And, you'd also better want to share it. If you don't, then your idea is not going to reach very many people or make you very successful. Don't be cocky, but be very confident and excited about yourself and your ideas. This enthusiasm is picked up by other people and, in many cases, they'll want to be a part of it.

The third tip is to always be adequately prepared to promote yourself, whatever your talent. This means you should get a business card, attend networking events, and create opportunities for success. Utilize every social media opportunity and connect with others at a similar place in life. Meet people on the internet and the "real world" who share your interests and who could help you in your quest for popularity and success.

Finally, don't be afraid to be a little edgy and even controversial. Brian Bosworth was a first round draft pick by the Seattle Seahawks of the National Football League. His football career was cut short due to injuries, but he knew how to get attention. He once flew into practice by helicopter. Was it brash and a little reckless? Yes. Did the national media jump all over it and make him a household name? Yes!

Later when the Seahawks played the Denver Broncos, Bosworth mouthed off about John Elway, Denver's popular quarterback. Broncos fans were so outraged that ten thousand of them bought fifteen dollar "Ban the Boz" T-shirts and wore them to the Seahawks game. It turns out Bosworth's company made the shirts. He got the last laugh and won big to the tune of 150,000 dollars (8)!

When doing stunts like Bosworth's, keep in mind that a popular person needs ethics (see Chapter 12). In the Bosworth examples, he didn't do anything unethical or illegal. Being outrageous isn't immoral or criminal, but if used properly, can put you on the fast track to becoming a local celebrity. Heck, my dad still tells me the story of an acquaintance from high school who drove ten miles to another town completely in reverse. Sure, it sounds stupid, but almost fifty years later he is still being mentioned in his hometown. Will your antics be remembered in fifty years?

So, get out there and start promoting yourself. For your practice assignment, I want you to find a networking event in your area. They can be found through internet search engines. Get some business cards, go to the meeting, approach others, and tell them about what you do. Lots of people come to networking events to meet others and share their products or businesses. They expect to be approached, so it's a low pressure environment.

I have a friend who got a better job through one of these

networking events and my business has benefited greatly from these contacts. Even the photo model for the chapter on body language (Chapter 33) came from a networking event. These opportunities could be yours if you go out and sell yourself.

CHAPTER 23

ASK AND YOU SHALL RECEIVE (MOST OF THE TIME)

Back in 2010, thanks to the dangerous combination of flip flops, a laundry basket, and carpeted stairs, my wife broke her ankle. She required surgery, but fortunately, the ankle healed nicely and she was able to resume normal activities. While she was still on crutches, my wife and I went out for coffee with my brother David and his wife. After we ordered our coffee, David pointed to my wife and asked the employee if we were eligible for the "cripple discount." The employee gave us a funny look and said, "We don't have that, but I can give you another discount." We received fifteen percent off our coffees.

That day I learned a valuable lesson, one so great that even Jesus taught it: ask and you shall receive. While Jesus was talking about asking God in prayer, I've noticed that what he says applies to many other situations as well. All too often, we do not get what we want from life because we are too afraid to ask. Sometimes, like in my experience with the coffee shop employee, it's possible to ask for and receive something that up until that point didn't even exist!

This chapter is closely related to my previous advice on self-promotion. I mentioned that if you don't promote yourself, then no one else is going to either. The same principle holds true for getting what you want, whether it's a better deal on car insurance or a chance to audition in front of a record producer. You'll never get any opportunities unless you take the initiative and ask.

Many times when you ask, the answer is going to be "no." This is, I believe, why so many people prefer not to even ask a question to begin with. We've conditioned ourselves to expect failure because we've had a negative response to so many of our questions in the past. In school, we'd ask to go to the bathroom only to be told by a negative teacher that we couldn't go twice in a day or we have an angry boss who always denies our raise request. And, let's face it, rejection hurts. As a result, we learned that it's best not to ask for something in the first place.

In my former teaching job, a colleague asked for more money when he signed a new contract, even though he had heard, like me, that asking for more money was fruitless. I'll never know what answer he received, but I give him credit for at least trying. After all, if he had to live with a lower paycheck, at least he could rest assured knowing that he made an effort to make more. I had to live with a low paycheck knowing that I made no effort to raise it!

As a celebrity in training, you must learn to ask, ask, and ask. If you have a need, ask for it. Heck, even if you have a want, ask for it. It could be as simple as a free refill for your drink or as advanced as an upgrade to first class on your flight to Sydney. The first rule is that if you don't ask, you'll never receive. If you want the amazing benefits of being a celebrity, then ask for them!

You also need to realize how to ask a question. One of the reasons so many people hear "no" all the time is because of the way they ask the question. They are gruff, whiny, or they make demands of people. You are not like that! A popular person will use humor, build rapport, and find other techniques to make the odds of "yes," or at least a compromise answer, a little better. In fact, if you're cool, most people will at least try to give you something, even if they have to tell you "no" to your original request.

Another good tip for receiving the answer you want is to ask in a way that shows you're meeting the needs of the other person. For example, a friend of mine needed my help chopping wood one afternoon. He told me that in return he'd help me clean up the leaves in my yard with his leaf blower. Although I would've helped him anyway, his efforts to meet my needs while asking me for help made me grateful and even excited about helping him. If you can offer someone a favor in return, they will be more likely to grant your request. Of course, if you promise something, make sure to follow through.

Once when I wanted a free refill at Starbucks (which they don't give), I asked the employee "Can you top off the coffee for your favorite customer?" I had built rapport with her, proven my value, and got her laughing. So, she told me not to tell anyone, but I got my refill.

Once, however, I tried the same line at a McDonald's and they wouldn't give me another iced coffee because it wasn't their policy. I heard the word "no." And that's fine. Whenever you ask for something, you have to be prepared for a negative answer. How do you take it? First, you are detached (Chapter 15). Not receiving whatever you asked for is not the end of the world. You have to remember that. Second, there's no failure, only feedback (Chapter 11). Maybe I could've worked the girl at McDonald's a little more with my routines and done more rapport building. On the other hand, maybe she'd given free drinks to her friends previously and her manager had been watching her like a hawk. Whatever the reason, it doesn't matter if you hear "no."

Keep in mind that a person who asks for stuff all the time becomes viewed as a sponge. You probably have friends like this and hate to be around them. Consequently, you never want people to think you are a mooch. This is why it's essential that you internalize the give-get-give mindset (see Chapter 8). Then, people will gladly accommodate you when you ask, because it's never done from a sense of entitlement. Think of the George Bailey example from the movie "It's a Wonderful Life." People happily helped his family out when they were in dire need because he had helped them and their loved ones many times previously. It may be fiction, but it illustrates a valuable point.

Your assignment for this chapter is to practice asking for things. Go out tonight and ask for something. It can be anything, even extra French fries at Burger King. Even if you just *know* you'll get a negative answer, ask anyway. I want you to notice two things. First, hearing the word "no" won't kill you and second, the answer won't often even be "no." You'd be amazed how flexible other people can be when asked nicely and with a sense of humor. So, when you ask, use all of the skills you've learned so far.

CHAPTER 24

HAVE A LITTLE MYSTERY

I love coffee. Can you tell from the other chapters? Sure, I'm addicted, but that's another story. I also love being out in public, so coffee shops are some of my favorite hangouts. At one coffee shop where I spend a lot of time, a young woman who worked there was always interested in what I did for a living. I was intentionally vague, so she would constantly guess about my career and status.

Because I carried books, she assumed I was a writer. I told her "Yes, I did some writing in my job." I once wore a shirt with Japan on it and she asked if I'd ever been to Japan. I told her jokingly "I'm big in Japan." Another time she asked if I was famous. I told her "Well, everyone here loves me, don't they?"

You notice how I didn't really answer any of her questions. As frustrating as it may have been for her, I did it on purpose. And, I might add, it had its desired effect. Every time I refused to answer, notice how she tried to fill in the blanks about me? She knew I was high value by the way I dressed, acted, and talked, so she naturally wanted to figure out why and how I'd become so attractive.

As a celebrity, you want to create a certain air of mystery about you. I'll emphasize it again: you don't want to lie about yourself or get others to think you're something you're obviously not. However, you also don't want to give away too much information all at once. The brain is actually wired to enjoying figuring out missing information. It's why humans love puzzles, trivia, and find images of barely clothed models titillating. Imagine "Jeopardy" or "Who Wants to Be A Millionaire?" if they were just a bunch of facts listed for thirty minutes. Neither would have made it to TV!

As you become popular, you can benefit from the brain's preference for mystery. It's a little like Christmas growing up. I'd see all those wrapped boxes and my brain would go wild with pleasure chemicals. I'd wonder what was in each box, hoping it was something cool. Unwrapping each present was incredibly pleasurable. Even if it ended up being boring underwear, the process itself was amazing. You should be the human equivalent of a nicely wrapped Christmas present. Other people should, when they meet you, feel excited about getting to know you in more depth.

The mistake most people make is to reveal too much at once or just too much in general. If your life is an open book to everyone you meet, you'll not only come on too strong, but you won't give anyone a reason to even follow up with you or get to know you better. You also will likely come across as generally boring since there is never any exciting sense of mystery or joy of discovery in knowing you.

In order to create an air of mystery, you'll have to follow two basic pieces of advice. The first is not to tell every single detail about yourself. This can actually be helpful when you're building a fan base because you may not be the most exciting or awesome person in the world at this moment. By being vague, you can avoid telling the cute girl you just met that you flip burgers at McDonald's.

I did this a lot when I was starting my business. I told people I was starting a business and they'd ask what it did. I'd say "what doesn't it do?" and leave it at that. Now that my business model is more established and well-defined, I am more direct. But, in the beginning, it allowed me to appear mysterious and keep me from having to explain that my business was still in the brainstorming and building stages.

My second tip is to do what I did with Stacy, the cute employee at the coffee shop. I got her to create a trans-derivational search, or TDS, about me. A TDS occurs when the person you're talking to tries to make sense of what you've just said. Our brain needs to make sense of the world, so it takes partial information and tries to make a complete picture of reality. However, if it doesn't have the complete picture, the brain has to fill in certain details.

If you're direct and detailed, there's no need for a TDS. However, if you're vague or elusive, you'll find your conversation partners creating a TDS, which you can use to your advantage.

For example, if you ask someone, "Remember that feeling you had last night?" it will lead to a "TDS" while the person determines what you were talking about. Was it the feeling of happiness after dinner or the feeling of anger at the power going out at midnight? Purposefully creating a TDS forces a person to pause and think, which interrupts his or her normal thought patterns. This puts people in a trance-like state and makes them open to suggestion and interaction with you. Signs of TDS are a pause, wide eyes, dilated pupils, slight confusion, etc. You're basically watching the person's thought processes at work.

If you want to create a TDS with someone, it's not hard. The best way is to be ambiguous. This is when you say words that can be taken in multiple ways. For example, if I say "The woman stabbed the boy with an umbrella" it can mean different things. It could mean a woman stabbed a boy who was holding an umbrella or a woman used an umbrella as a weapon to stab the boy. I used ambiguity with Stacy successfully. By telling her "I'm big in Japan" she had to wonder whether I was kidding and even if I wasn't, what does being big in Japan mean anyway? A direct answer would've been "My wife bought this shirt for me at the airport during a stopover in Japan as a present." However, that doesn't sound nearly as awesome, now does it?

Why would you want to get someone to create a trans-derivational search anyway? Ultimately you want to generate a TDS to get others to fill in the blanks about you in a positive way. Even though I'm a cool, popular, and successful guy, when I let Stacy create a version of me in her mind, I guarantee what she came up with was far superior to even my great reality. She made positive assumptions about me and viewed me even more highly afterward. And, I didn't even have to reveal any real information about myself.

Still, you don't just want to just play with someone's mind, although this can be fun. You ultimately want to get each person to assume something positive or mysterious about you. For example, if you walk into a crowded place and say, "I think a lot of people here would benefit from my business," people are going to assume that you run a business. Maybe you do, and it's selling Star Wars figurines on EBay. However, people will hear "business" and probably fill in the blanks in a positive fashion. They may ask themselves, "What does he do? Does he make a lot of money?" and so on.

A TDS is typically formed positively or negatively based on the mood or situation of the people you're talking to. This makes sense if you think about it. They are not basing their opinion of you on actual facts, but on their own assumptions about who they think you are (or want you to be). If they're happy and in a good mood, they're likely to assume good things. This is even more true if you're the one who has put them in a good mood! So, make sure you've shown your sense of humor and high value before trying to generate a TDS. Then they'll assume the best about you.

Keep in mind that while mystery is important, there are times when being mysterious or vague isn't appropriate. If you're at a networking meeting, for example, you probably need to be more direct about what you do, or people will assume you either do nothing valuable or you're flaky. The same is true if you're pulled over by a cop. If he asks for license and registration, you'd better just do it. Use common sense about when to be mysterious, and when to be more straightforward.

Your assignment is to write down ways that you can be more mysterious on a regular basis. Remember, the goal isn't to lie or mislead, just to create ambiguity. Look at my examples from the first paragraph for ways to be more mysterious. Also, the best way to be more mysterious instantly is to simply not talk about yourself in great detail around others. No one really wants to hear your life story anyway!

CHAPTER 25

ARE YOU PAYING ATTENTION?

One of the funniest experiences I had while teaching was when preparing my students for a test. I typically played review games with them, which they loved. During one game, I tried to emphasize that a particular topic I thought was important would be on the test. I told the kids three times in no uncertain terms that they would be tested on this question. A week later, as I was handing back the graded tests, one young man who had played the review game complained about missing the very question I had told them to prepare for. When I told him the answer and asked him why he didn't study it, he looked at me and said in complete earnestness, "I didn't think it would even be on the test!"

As I mentioned when I talked about mindfulness in Chapter 15, most people go through life in a semi-aware state. They glide from event to event with little concern for the details in between. In most cases, this also includes living in a fog of unawareness. It's sad, but most humans are unconcerned with their surroundings or even with their own mental state. Lack of awareness is a huge problem. Think about all the problems that could be prevented if everyone simply paid more attention: medical errors, car accidents, late arrivals, financial market bubbles and crashes, and so on.

A Buddhist monk once asked his teacher to write down the fundamental tenet of Buddhism. The master wrote "attention" on the parchment. The student disliked the answer, thinking there had to be more. He pressed his teacher further who finally relented. He wrote "attention, attention, attention."

I love this story because I truly believe that success in life is mostly about paying attention. You pay attention to the world around you and you can anticipate needs and problems. You pay attention to trends and you can get in on opportunities at the ground level. You pay attention to people and you can learn the ways to win them over, meet their needs, and get them to do what you want. You pay attention to details and you will always be able to outsmart the rest of the world, which is happy to live in oblivious ignorance.

For someone wanting to be popular and famous, paying attention is key. Look at the example I gave in Chapter 21 when I discussed the origins of rock and roll. Not only were the early pioneers of rock music breaking from the herd, but they were paying attention to the dissatisfaction many people had with the direction music was going. Behind every celebrity or successful person is someone who paid attention to a need or a trend and jumped on it before everyone else finally woke up to the opportunity.

A popular guy will find paying attention to be one of the best weapons in his arsenal of popularity. This is due to a sad fact of society: most people don't get much attention. With the rise of single parenthood, day cares, nursing homes, sixty hour work weeks, etc. most people have never gotten the attention they need to be happy and well-adjusted. And, in most cases, even as adults, they're still not getting it!

You can capitalize on the loneliness epidemic that is crushing America. By taking an interest in people, actively listening to them, and giving them your attention, they will then value you because you're meeting one of their core needs. This is why you shouldn't ever feel like you're "exploiting" lonely people by using the techniques in this book. You're not taking advantage of anyone. There is a deep need (relationships) that most Americans (and those in other places) are not getting met and you, as a smart celebrity, know that you are giving your time and getting something (a celebrity status) in return.

Another reason why a popular person must learn to pay attention is that it makes you look extremely high value. Keep in mind that being wise and looking smart are really about paying attention. If you do well in school it's because you pay attention to what you're learning. If you're a great actor, it's because you've paid attention so well in real life that you can effectively model it on the screen or the stage. A great businessman paid attention to a need and made millions. You get it?

Whenever I go out and meet people, my paying attention skills are always on display, and they help me become more and more popular. Let me give you an outline of a typical encounter. When I enter a place, I pay attention to body language, so (unless I am in a particularly daring mood) I approach people who are open to interaction with me. When I talk to them, I use observational humor related to details in the environment or in the news (more paying attention). If it's a girl, I tease her a little about some detail of her clothing. Finally, I read the situation to determine if the person is interested enough to want my contact information.

You see how my whole evening was spent paying attention? My success started with paying attention, continued through paying attention, and ended by paying attention. It's also possible to argue that much of my general success comes from paying attention. Heck, I even wrote this book because of all the men and women who told me they needed help in making friends and getting dates. I paid attention to their words and their needs. It's like the Buddhist master said "attention, attention, attention."

Your practice is to re-read all of Chapter 15 and re-do that assignment. I'm guessing that you're not as mindful or detached as you should be. Being mindful and detached are the two mental keys to successfully paying attention and using that to your advantage to achieve popularity. This is because if you're preoccupied or living in the past or the future, you'll never be able to pay attention (and be successful) in the present.

Chapter 26

Risky Business

I absolutely hate poison ivy. I'm not generally a hater (of plants or otherwise), but I'm terribly allergic to its oil. So, I try to avoid it like the plague, otherwise I have so many red spots all over my body, I look like I have the plague. One summer while I was hiking with friends at one of Ohio's state parks, we decided to go down a new path. It was great for the first mile, but then the path narrowed and there was poison ivy along the sides of the trail. Normally I would've turned back. In fact, I started to turn around.

However, my friends told me to just continue walking. I countered that it was risky. They told me the path could be really awesome and that was worth the risk. I took a few deep breaths, put one foot in front of the other, and continued on the trail. They were right: the route was absolutely stunning. It took us by an abandoned road that had since been reclaimed by nature. It was incredibly cool to see a rusted out antique car in the middle of the woods. Every summer, I make it a point to hike that amazing trail. Oh, and I haven't gotten any poison ivy on my skin there. Not even once.

There has been some scientific research on the topic of regrets. One study showed that while humans tend to regret both actions they've done and failed to do, the most long term regret usually focuses on missed opportunities (9). In other words, the most emotionally damaging form of regret is when we fail to take advantage of (or create) an opportunity that is no longer possible (like dating a long gone high school crush). Since another study notes adults spend on average forty-five minutes a week dwelling on their regrets (10), failing to act in certain situations can leave a person with a lifelong emotional toll.

When we want to act in some way, but fail to do so, it usually comes down to one word (in spite of various excuses): fear. In some cases feeling fear can be a very good thing. For example, if we decide we'd like to wade across a creek and see an alligator, fear of death or serious harm will likely make us look upstream for a bridge. However, in many cases, our desire to act is stopped by an irrational fear called "anxiety." Irrational anxiety is never a good thing and is one of the biggest contributors to regret. Sometimes we "play it safe" simply because we fear taking a good risk that could have incredible rewards.

My recommendation, if you want to become popular and successful is to take reasonable, educated, and safe (RES) risks and do so frequently. I am a naturally cautious person, which has served me well in some ways. I've never tried drugs and I have no credit card debt. Yet, I live with a lot of "what if" type of regrets.

I realize that while being cautious with chemicals and avoiding debt are good traits, being cautious with other aspects of life (like self-promotion) may not be. Consequently, one of my declarations (see Chapter 2) is to take at least one good risk every single day. And, I follow through on it. I've still avoided doing stupid things, but my life is more adventurous and abundant. Hold on, though. Before you go out and do something dumb that will get you in trouble, finish reading the rest of this chapter!

First, I want to define the kind of risk that I think you should take. I'm talking about a "good" risk, one that has a lot of upside and doesn't put you or other people in serious danger. This risk, once again, is reasonable, educated, and safe (RES). Most of the risks that lead to problems are "bad" risks. They have very little upside and put the person taking them and others in danger. They are irrational, show little foresight, and are unsafe. For clarity, I'm going to examine each aspect of a good risk in more detail.

The first aspect of a good risk is that it is reasonable (R). This means that you've thought about the risk and weighed the pros and cons (see next paragraph). The reward should always be worth the risk. For example, "investing" your money in thousands of lottery tickets, when you know the odds of getting struck by lightning are better, probably isn't rational. Part of being reasonable is that the outcome also has to be possible for you to achieve. Becoming president of the firm where you work at age thirty is possible. Becoming president of the United States at thirty (barring a change in the Constitution) is genuinely impossible.

The second aspect of a good risk is that it is educated (E). This means that you've researched the upside (reward) and the downside of the risk. Then, you can make an informed decision about whether to take the risk. Maybe you were asked to put some money into a business venture and you looked up the company, did background checks on the owners, and so on. This is doing due diligence and should be done, when possible, with every risk you take. Sometimes researching the facts can be tough because you have to make a decision quickly (like whether or not to approach a girl with a jacked boyfriend beside her). In this case, you may have to go with your gut instinct or what you've learned in the past.

Finally, a good risk must always be safe (S). I don't mean that a risk is easy or comfortable. It's not going to be either or it wouldn't, by definition, be a risk. By safe, I mean it's not going to cause harm (physical or otherwise) to you or someone else. This is perhaps the most important part of a "good' risk. Most people will recover from stupid and irrational risks. However, many people die, go to jail, or develop a host of other problems based on a stupid *and* unsafe decision.

Is parking on the grass worth it? Some risks don't provide much reward in return for the possible consequences.

I also want to note that you can't let anxiety masquerade as any of these legitimate concerns. Let's look at the risk of starting your own business. Anxiety can tell you it's irrational because the economy's bad. Anxiety can tell you that all the evidence that your idea to make money is great – is really false. Anxiety can also tell you that starting your own business is unsafe because if you fail it will cause your family to starve. Anxiety sucks! So, don't let it cloud your thinking when deciding to take risks.

If anxiety threatens to hamper your success, talk yourself through the three parts of a good risk. Let's use the above example to show why anxiety is a nuisance when it tries to stop you from starting your own business. Being an entrepreneur is very reasonable. People start new businesses every day. Also, while many will fail, many also succeed. If you've done the research and are ready to put in the hard work, you clearly have a good chance of succeeding. Also, while feeding your family is a genuine concern, if you have a safety net of some kind and make wise business decisions, it's highly unlikely (especially in the United States of America) that your family will starve. Take note of how anxiety nearly stopped a hypothetical good risk and also how it's possible to "talk down" anxiety induced doubt.

I'm going to give a few examples of good and bad risks and break them down by categories:

Good risk- You want to take up a new exercise program even though you're out of shape

-Rational- Absolutely

-Educated- Sure, as long as you are healthy and check with a doctor

-Safe- While exercising can always be a risk, if you're cleared by a doctor, it will actually make you healthier!

Good risk- Getting back in the dating game after a divorce

-Rational- Yes, a desire for human companionship is normal

-Educated- Just make sure you don't go after a pyscho

-Safe- Yes, but avoid the girl with an ax collection

Bad risk- Investing in a person who won't reveal any financial history

-Rational- No; financial disclosure is accepted business practice

-Educated- If you don't know his background, it can't be educated

-Safe- For your money and welfare, probably not

Bad risk- Drunk Driving

-Rational- No, considering the possible consequences

-Educated- Law enforcement can give some horrible examples of drunk driving accidents; can result in death or jail

-Safe- No. Can lead to death or serious injury for self or others

Hopefully, you can see what constitutes a good risk and a bad risk. Notice how the good risks are all difficult, perhaps stress-inducing tasks, but also have the reward of making you popular, healthier, or more successful. Also, notice how the bad risks may give you short term benefits (for example, driving drunk may save you the hassle of waiting on a taxi or a friend), but have serious downsides, not only short term (like a wrecked car), but also long term (vehicular homicide can carry steep prison time).

In my career at a substance abuse counseling agency, I see the results of bad choices every day: addiction, STD's, criminal records, overdose deaths, etc. Bad risks can have serious consequences and really can ruin lives. However, good risks (like starting a business) can also have great rewards. Just make sure your risks are rational, educated, and safe (RES) and you will find they usually pay off. And, if they don't, they won't leave you worse off than when you started.

Your assignment for this chapter is to write out four "good" risks you can take over the next four days. Write out the risk, then fill in the details for each category (rational, educated, and safe). If you determine that it's rational, educated, safe and beneficial for your quest for popularity, then go out and do it. And, don't let anxiety stop you from doing it. You also may consider adding "taking a good risk each day" to your declarations (see Chapter 2).

CHAPTER 27

IT'S ALL ABOUT RELATIONSHIPS

I've learned, ever since I've been young, the importance of relationships. My dad, an executive at several substance abuse counseling centers, modeled this great wisdom. He constantly took calls from friends, high government officials, and others in the community who needed his advice for themselves or people they loved. He always responded with his time and energy. They, out of gratitude, then helped him in any way that they could. He is successful and beloved. Every now and again, he'd remind me the secret of his success: "it's all about relationships."

Those words have stuck with me throughout the years. Dad makes great efforts to start and nurture positive relationships and finds great financial and social success from such a mentality. However, I've also seen the opposite side of the coin. Several people I went to high school with left town as soon as they could and even made an active effort to sever long held relationships.

Although I can't blame people for wanting to start over, obliterating your social network doesn't seem to be a smart move, especially since the adage "it's not what you know, but who you know" remains even more true than ever. With a poor economy and deteriorating social conditions in most of the Western world, knowing the right people has become essential. This is especially true if you want to be popular.

People become famous and loved because they make the right impressions upon a large number of people. I promise you there is not a celebrity alive who has not gotten a break by knowing someone connected. In fact, I've read countless interviews where celebrities "made it" when they encountered the right person at the right time. However, this wasn't just dumb luck. Their success never would've happened without a strong effort at forming real and beneficial relationships.

The best way to benefit from relationships is to create new ones and maintain the ones you have. You can follow the tips laid out later in this book to approach, build rapport, and then make the close to expand your social circle (Chapters 36, 37, and 38). To maintain the friends you have, the best method is to, surprise, pay attention to them on a regular basis. My good friend Joshua Wagner likes to interact with at least five people a day on Facebook. David and I make it a point to at least wish all of our contacts a "happy birthday" on Facebook. Another tip would be to call or text at least one friend from your contact list daily. Whatever you choose, what matters most is that you make an effort to cultivate friendships on a regular basis.

Another tip is to never, ever, discount the smaller connections you've made. I have over nine hundred Facebook friends and sometimes I'll get asked if I'm really friends with all of them. A lot of commentators would answer that it's impossible. Their reasoning basically assumes you can't really be friends with that many people. I agree with that assumption if we're talking about deep friendships. However, from a social networking standpoint, having over nine hundred Facebook friends is a blessing. Even the smallest contact could provide a huge benefit, especially if that person likes you and values your talents.

A few months ago, a girl I know deactivated her Facebook account because she was having problems with her boyfriend. Rather than having access to her previous five hundred or so contacts, she now has her family and local friends. If someone on her list has an opportunity for business, free concert tickets, or anything else beneficial, guess who's not going to get it? In fact, when I was trying to find cover models for another book, I originally thought of her. Of course, when she deactivated I had no way of contacting her!

That's why I always tell people that unless you are being harassed, don't delete contacts from your phone or your social networking circle.

You never know when even the smallest opportunity could pay off. I've gotten a graphic designer and a model (for this book) from friends on my social network. In addition, I've offered friends I've kept in contact with through Facebook opportunities in my own business. The girl who deactivated? She won't be appearing in any of my books at this time.

I want to end this chapter by telling you a little more about my dad and the benefits he receives from forging close friendships with other people, especially people in high places. His agency gets constant referrals from networking contacts. If he needs anything he can almost always make a phone call and get it. If he runs into problems, he knows the right person to contact to get it resolved immediately. I remember as a child traveling to Wisconsin and having the county sheriff tell dad to call day or night if he ran into any issues! That impressed me.

I too have found many of the benefits that come from forging relationships. However, it's worth remembering that popularity requires both giving and taking. I receive the benefits (like my dad) of relationships because I offer those people something to begin with. They, in turn, give of themselves in any way they can. Don't simply look at relationships in terms of what you can take. Building true relationships requires a lot of giving and is always a two way street.

Your assignment is to interact with five friends on your social network right now. It only takes a few minutes, so you should make a habit of doing this each day. The more you interact with your contacts, even in small ways, the more likely they will think of you when they have opportunities or help you if the time comes. If you don't have any social media contacts, then you'd better get on Facebook or another site and get some right now. In this day and age, if you want to be truly popular, you'll need a social media presence.

CHAPTER 28

THE ROCK STAR PROBLEM (?)

If you want to see a detailed look at the lives of celebrities, all you have to do is check out celebrity gossip magazines and tabloids. Although I don't buy them, they're hard to miss while standing in line at the grocery store. The glamour of the celebrity lifestyle is obvious: designer clothes, hanging with and dating the beautiful people, the multimillion dollar homes and expensive toys. Who wouldn't want all that?

However, the magazines also reveal a darker side of being famous. They show the constant hounding by the press, the prying into private affairs, the celebrity stalkers, and the many temptations (like extreme drug abuse) that can come with fame. Being a celebrity can be insanely awesome, but, especially for those who aren't mentally predisposed for it, it can also be insane. The high profile overdoses, suicides, and burnouts in the celebrity crowd are a good indicator.

Unless you make it to the big, big time, you probably won't have to deal with the extreme forms of the problems I just mentioned. Yet, even locally popular people have headaches to deal with from time-to-time. Being popular and having fans is a blast! But I'd be lying if I said there wasn't a possibility that negative issues will arise. I've included this chapter so you'll have a realistic view of popularity's downside and be able to cope with it if and when it comes.

Here are some of the most common problems you'll face as you become more popular. Note these are not always problems in and of themselves. For example, a celebrity loves being recognized and cheered on when he's on the red carpet, but being recognized and cheered on when he's trying to finish his grocery shopping in peace is a little different.

Speaking of being recognized, the first problem you may face is lack of privacy. The more people you know and interact with, the better the chances you will be noticed when you're in public. When I was a teacher, I was so popular with my teenage students that they always came and visited me in my classroom and elsewhere around the school. I loved their company. But, when I was trying to get work done or just needed a break, their constant visits could be exhausting.

Being attractive also means that some people will want your

attention in more extreme ways. While being stalked isn't terribly common, it can happen. If you are a woman, this can be even more dangerous. However, guys can have stalkers too. It's just something to be aware of. Obviously, if stalking and harassment become an issue, you may need to get law enforcement involved.

Finally, when people see your confidence and your success, they will want your help and services in a variety of capacities. This could vary depending on your career, interests, etc., but be aware that people will, in a genuine way, want you to help them, listen to them, or advocate for them. This could be little hassles like putting in a good word with a friend, or bigger annoyances like those who would try to mooch off your success and maybe even ask for your money. Resist the urge to give in to ridiculous and extravagant demands, even from good friends and family.

If you find yourself having these problems, don't fret. Unless it's a dangerous situation like a stalker, you know how to deal with the hassles of popularity. Act according to the principles you've learned in this book. So, you'll handle each problem with detachment, charm, flexibility, and especially assertiveness. Make your responses ethical and within your moral boundaries too.

The best piece of advice is to master saying "no" in a friendly, but firm way (see Chapter 18 for a review on how to do this). With most people, that will stop the pestering and you won't have lost a fan in the process. On the other hand, if you can't say "no" without being rude and aggressive, you will get them to leave you alone, probably permanently.

There isn't any real practice from this section because the rock star problem is probably not something you've encountered yet. Just keep it in the back of your mind and be ready to deal with it like a true celebrity when it arises. Because trust me, if you become popular, it will at some point. However, in most situations, the "problem" of being popular isn't a bad one to have.

CHAPTER 29

ONLINE POPULARITY

I have a Facebook friend whose life is an open book and it's up there with the best (or worst, depending on your perspective) celebrity gossip magazine. Her many friends and I are constantly deluged with her anxieties and her hatred (and extreme love) of whatever man she happens to be stuck on at that moment. We also learn which other people, some of whom are also her Facebook friends, are infuriating her and why they are idiots. While her wall is interesting to say the least, it's more "train wreck" interesting than "I want to get to know you" interesting.

On the other hand, my good friend Joshua Wagner has an awesome Facebook wall. He never whines, posts funny (and original) updates all the time; and he always has his friends coming over to comment on his statuses and ask how he's doing. He has a lot of contacts and his wall is a popular place to hang out in the virtual world. In fact, he has over a couple thousand Facebook friends.

With social media becoming so important to success, you have to not only act like a celebrity in the real world, but you must also carefully manage your online image as well. Chances are, the more popular you become in real life, the more people will want to connect with you online. For men and women under thirty, it's becoming the primary way to stay in contact. And, the older demographic is increasingly on Facebook and other social media as well. So, you have to keep up the same popular image there as you do in the real world.

Sadly, some people who are cool in real life think that when they get online they can be creepy, rude, whiny, or a host of other unattractive traits, all because they don't have to actually deal with another human being in person. Go to any comments section of a popular news article to see the low value nastiness in action. Remember, if you want to be popular and have fans, you have to be popular and cool in every setting, including when you use online social media.

Basically, make sure you follow the advice in this book whenever you're online. In other words, be flexible, fun, detached, funny, etc. not only when you see people in person, but also when you interact with them on your wall, through text, on internet comboxes, and so on. Remember to be patient too, since lots of men and women think being online gives them permission to act differently. Don't get sucked into their drama. Being anonymous (or nearly so) can't be a reason to undo all of the hard work you're putting in to better yourself in the "real" world.

Here are a few tips for behaving online, many of which come from the fertile mind of David Bennett. Follow them and you will be as successful and popular on the internet as you are in other environments.

-Don't put yourself down, unless it is an obvious joke (e.g. a bodybuilder joking about being skinny)

-If you're a guy, don't act like a girl, or broadcast your love for girly things. Look at the types of things your female friends are saying, and the way they say it. Don't do it. I've seen many men get "friend zoned" due to overly emotional Facebook behavior (see Chapter 34).

-Don't broadcast your failures. Don't be the person who advertises when they experience romantic rejection or the one who is always whining about being single. Keep it to yourself or you will have more lost friends to whine about.

-Don't get too political, religious, activistic, etc. You don't have to be bland, but you also don't want to be the person that everybody ignores because every post is about some pet issue.

-Don't be online all the time. Show the world that you are successful, have hobbies, etc., outside of watching a screen refresh. Take a few days off social media occasionally (unannounced) to keep your friends guessing.

-Don't say weird, sexual, or violent things. Don't talk about pornography, killing things (except legal hunting), bodily functions, your hatred of women or men, etc.

-Don't play games all day. Nothing says low value like having a profile page all filled with game updates. It suggests you don't work and don't have a social life.

-Don't be creepy. Don't add strangers as friends, or people you barely know, and don't "hover" around someone online, just as you wouldn't hover around them in public.

-Don't whine, complain, or play the victim. The world is already too whiny. This will turn people away from you very quickly.

-Don't overtly broadcast your successes too often or people will think you're arrogant or insecure. Work your high value accomplishments in indirectly or with humor. For example, you could say, "the funniest thing happened today on my run..." That advertises that you ran, a real accomplishment, but it's not the main focus on the post or obvious bragging.

-Be funny and entertaining, but originally so. In other words, don't repeat other people's jokes. Most of your friends will be able to spot "canned" material a mile away.

-Be friendly and encouraging to a diverse group of friends. Say happy birthday, "like" a variety of people's statuses, etc. However, change things up regularly, so you aren't stalking one or two profiles.

In other words, keep as many people in your loop as possible.

-Post on diverse things. Be the one with multiple interests who is always doing and saying something new and exciting. This makes you attractive to a wide variety of people. For example, I post about working out, networking, my business, going out with family, etc. Anyone following my profile can see that I am well-rounded.

-Be patient. Respond to friend requests, comments, etc., when you want to respond. There is no need to reply the minute or even day after, since you are successful and busy (or should be).

-Know when to give up. Exit a fruitless, aggressive, etc., discussion. There is no shame in bowing out if a discussion is beneath you. You may even wish to assertively make this known. It's probably best not to engage these types of discussions to begin with.

-Be mysterious. There is nothing wrong with being a little vague. Even if you aren't as successful or popular as you want to be, make people think you are! But, don't go so far as to lie. Eventually it will catch up with you and you'll have some explaining to do (see Chapter 24).

Today your assignment is to "revamp" your social media websites. If you have a blog with your real name attached to it, go and delete the obnoxious, creepy, or low value posts. Better yet, close it down and start a new one. Go on your Facebook profile and edit your interests, jobs, inspiring figures, etc. to reflect the new high-value you. If your wall is filled with games, delete them. Even better, stop playing and devote that time to finding multimillion dollar ideas, exercising, or promoting yourself. Change your profile photos if necessary to reflect the new you. Get rid of the pics with your gut sticking out, or the ones where you are making the duck-face, and put up something classy. You get the picture. Reboot your Facebook, MySpace, Twitter, etc. identity right now.

If you think you must whine, vent, or engage in pointless discussion, find a totally anonymous forum and let it loose. I would argue, however, that as you mature and grow as a popular person you will find little desire to waste your time on such fruitlessness.

CHAPTER 30

CENTER OF GRAVITY

One day, my brother David and I walked into a Tim Horton's coffee shop in Columbus. We put on the popularity charm extra strong and had the girl at the register practically eating from our hand. However, something interesting happened. Her co-workers stopped working (fortunately it wasn't a busy day) and came over and inserted themselves into the conversation. Not only that, but a customer even got up from his table and joined in the conversation.

It was an amazing sight. David and I were standing at the counter surrounded by about six people all hanging on our every word and hoping to join in! That day we encountered what we at The Popular Man call "celebrity gravity," which is what happens when you become popular: you have a way of drawing others closer to you. And it works exponentially. The more people are interested in you, the greater the chance that even larger numbers will want to be with you.

This is illustrated by a psychological phenomenon called social proof, which is covered in <u>Influence</u> by Robert Cialdini (which I mentioned earlier and which you should have bought!). Basically, if other people like a person or a product, then you are more likely to appreciate it as well. You see this in advertising all the time through endorsements, whether from celebrities or average people. It works like a charm because it makes us feel comfortable in our choices. It's basically peer pressure, except without overt pressure.

In the realm of people and relationships, social proof works much the same way. People see you surrounded by others and subconsciously make several positive assumptions about you. First, they know that you are safe and approachable. You're not going to kill or harm them because others are obviously talking to you and surviving just fine. Second, it proves you are worth knowing. If you are holding the attention of five people, then you must be interesting. If you are holding the attention of thousands or millions of people then you must be extremely interesting (then you become a true celebrity).

Just as the sun's gravity attracts the planets, you should attract people to you.

Social proof was demonstrated through an experiment several years ago, which Cialdini references. Social scientists asked a person to stand on a busy city street and look at the sky. The vast majority of people simply walked on by. However, when scientists asked several people to look up at the sky, then a large number of bystanders stopped and also looked at the sky together. They assumed that one lone person wasn't worth their effort. But, if a crowd thought it was important to look up, then those walking by thought they had better look up as well. This is an important lesson for anyone wanting to become more popular. After all, popularity and fame are ultimately a numbers game.

There are several ways to use social proof to your advantage as you pursue popularity. If you are a high value person, then this gravity will happen naturally. A smart, witty, outgoing, good looking person who shares these traits with the world will attract others to his side. You just have to get out, approach others, and let the gravity happen. Believe me, it works with little effort, except to be your normal excellent self.

You can also use your available resources to give yourself social proof. If you have a lot of friends, then bring them out with you in public, get them laughing and showing how much they like you, and then bring strangers into your group. The same is true if you're a guy looking for dates. Find some of your best looking female friends and take them out to clubs or other venues with you. Even though you may have no intention of dating those women, it still makes you look popular to be surrounded by beautiful women.

One man even created social proof from nothing. Brett Cohen, a student, hired body guards, groupies, and even paparazzi as an experiment in social engineering. Sure enough, by acting like a celebrity and, most importantly, paying others to treat him like a celebrity, people off the street assumed he was famous! They asked for his autograph, took his picture, and generally wanted his time (11). This is celebrity gravity in action, even if it is "fake." Nonetheless, he still received a write up in a major British newspaper, so maybe lasting fame isn't that far around the corner for Mr. Cohen.

If you have trouble getting a crowd to form around you (and don't want to pay for one), then remember that most people just want to enjoy life. The vast majority of men and women either hate or are indifferent to their lives, which are filled with meaningless work, dysfunctional relationships, and lots of stress. They would love to enter into an enjoyable reality. If you can provide that by making them laugh, giving them positive attention, and meeting their emotional needs, then they will come to you.

This is exactly what happened to David and me at Tim Horton's. Anyone working in service can tell you that most customers suck. They complain and whine or are just unremarkable and faceless. We made someone feel so good and laugh so much that day that all the employees and even a customer wanted to be a part of our magic. If you go out and give the world laughter, joy, and fun, you too will have gravity wherever you are.

Your assignment for this chapter is to engage in some people watching. Go out to a crowded place and play a little game: find the popular person. It's usually not hard. Look for the men and women who have a bunch of people around them. Watch the interaction among everyone involved. Also, notice how even strangers seem to be attracted to the action, even if it's just through smiling when they walk by. Write down what you observed and think about how you can use it in your own life.

CHAPTER 31

BE CONTAGIOUS!

In the early 90's my family and I took a trip to Columbus, Ohio to watch their "Red, White, and Boom" fireworks display. We stayed at the Hyatt hotel downtown. It just happened that Alfonso Ribeiro, at the height of his fame for his work on the television show "The Fresh Prince of Bel Aire" was also staying in the same hotel. I discovered this while I was in the same elevator with him (along with some screaming preteen girls).

I remember nothing else about that stay except for activities that related to Mr. Ribeiro. In addition to seeing him in the elevator, I also spent at least half of my first day trying find him. I did, at a party in the hotel's lobby, and got my picture taken with him. I still have the photo.

Although the details of my preteen encounter with this celebrity have faded somewhat, I still vividly recall the intense excitement I felt when I met him.

I don't think you need my story to realize that celebrities can create a level of excitement that is unmatched by ordinary people. Meeting a celebrity, for many people, would be considered a "peak experience" as described by psychologist Abraham Maslow. "Peak experiences" are intense moments of excitement, joy, wonder and awe. For most people, peak experiences define their lives in ways that normal experiences do not. This is why everyone remembers meeting someone famous or where they were on September 11th, 2001 but can't tell you what they had for lunch twelve days ago.

I know I've mentioned it a lot already, but most people simply don't have a lot of fun and excitement in their lives, which is why peak experiences are so meaningful and defining. Meeting famous people, going through coming of age rituals, taking great vacations, and going to concerts are examples of peak experiences. These events are memorable and meaningful. Part of the reason we treasure and value them so much is because they also tend to be rare.

As a popular person, it is your job to create mini peak experiences wherever you go. At this point, meeting you probably isn't going to be a life-changing event. However, it should be a day-changing event at the very least. Your goal should be to make life more exciting and more interesting for everyone you come into contact with.

Another interesting aspect of peak experiences is that they can change people's outlook, even if temporarily. Growing up I always wondered why every day couldn't be as special as Christmas. You know how it is: beautiful lights, wonderful decorations, a spirit of goodwill and joy, even among people who would normally bite your head off. When I asked adults the question, they would always answer that Christmas would no longer be special if we acted like it was Christmas all year long. How limiting! I guess, according to the world, we can't be happy and joyful 365 (or 366) days a year.

As a celebrity, you must get into the mindset that every day is Christmas. Each day you wake up is exciting and special. You're alive, you're popular and the world is yours for the taking. Your options are limitless. Are you excited yet? Well, you should be! Before I transformed my life, started my own business, and regained my youthful popularity, I used to love Christmas so much. However, now I enjoy Christmas, but it's not that special anymore. This is because I live an exciting, happy life every single day. I wake up with the excitement of knowing that every day is like Christmas. Why? Because I create memorable experiences with other people each day of my life.

Once you're excited and happy about life, your goal is to go out and share that excitement. Believe me, it's extremely contagious. Go into a stuffy place and start smiling. People may think you're weird at first, but eventually others will start smiling too. I guarantee it. It's because deep down everyone craves these joyful experiences. All people want to feel good, and if you give them the opportunity, they will join in. And love you for it. It's what being popular is all about.

However, some days you may not be the most exciting and upbeat person. To create contagious excitement, you may have to pump yourself up when you go out in public. Some people find listening to music or watching certain clips on YouTube helpful. Others pump themselves up through other means like exciting self-talk. Personally, I don't even need any special techniques anymore. I get excited enough just by the thought of being me. You may think I'm arrogant, but if you do this popularity thing for a few months, you'll know exactly what I mean.

Once you become joyful, happy, and excited, you must go out and interact positively with everyone you encounter, from the paperboy delivering your morning newspaper to the cashier at Wal-Mart ringing up your late night snack. You'll run into sour individuals who may scoff at you, but the vast majority of people will find your attitude infectious and your excitement extremely contagious. In most cases, they will want to join in.

A word of caution is needed before you go out and end up annoying the world. You don't want to be Buddy the Elf after ingesting a bottle of maple syrup (if you don't know this movie reference, do a YouTube search). You don't want to be so peppy and optimistic that you drive people crazy. Being authentically energetic, fun, witty, and happy (in the right dose) is more than enough.

Your assignment for this chapter is to record a "morning blitz" of your affirmations. The easiest way is to use your cell phone. Write down a few short affirmations (they can be the same as your earlier ones or shorter variants) like "You are excited, happy, and ready for a great day." Then, record your script on your cell phone or another recorder. Play it first thing every morning. Maybe even make it the tone for your cell phone alarm. I've been doing this for a while and even on days where I may feel a little tired initially, hearing my morning blitz gets me in the right state to go out and act like a celebrity: excited about life and spreading that excitement to others. And, it happens before I even have a chance to really wake myself up.

CHAPTER 32

TIME IS MONEY (OR SHOULD BE)

Awhile back I saw a video of people waiting in a line at a popular fast food restaurant. Except this was no ordinary line. It stretched outside of the restaurant onto the sidewalk and even wound around two city blocks. The reporter noted that the people in question were standing in line up to two hours to get...wait for it...a free hamburger! I couldn't believe what a colossal waste of time this was: waiting in line two hours for a dollar-fifty sandwich. They could've gotten the burger where it wasn't free, paid the buck-fifty, then used the remaining one hour and fifty five minutes to make a nice profit, even if working minimum wage. Instead they gave two hours of their life to save less than two lousy bucks.

Reading MJ DeMarco's <u>Millionaire Fastlane</u> completely changed my outlook on life (and you should be reading it!). He notes that rich people are generous with their money, but stingy with their time. Poor people are usually generous with their time, but not their money. What he means is that people who give hours each day to work menial jobs, watch sports, play video games, and stand in line to save a couple bucks, will almost always end up poor. On the other hand, those individuals who use their time executing great ideas and promoting themselves will end up very rich.

It makes sense if you think about it. Your most valuable asset is your time. Money is pretty much unlimited with a government printing press, while you are limited in time to twenty four hours a day, seven days a week, 365 days a year. And, even if you're very lucky, you'll likely get one hundred of those years. You can't change time no matter how much you whine, complain, or beg your Maker. And, since that time is scarce, it is extremely valuable. Or it should be.

However, look at how most people treat their time. They give sixty hours a week to a job they hate so they can buy a slightly nicer car to impress their neighbors. They spend five hours a day building up virtual farms on Facebook or being wizards in alternate universes. Or they laze on a couch all day and then sleep in until noon on the weekends. Given the limitations and value of time, it's amazing how much people actually spend completely wasting it (or sleeping it away)!

Truly successful people know the truth about time. It's your greatest asset. If you use your time to come up with great ideas, network with other people, build your brand, promote yourself, or pursue your dreams, you will achieve the freedom and success that your "virtual farmer" friend or your neighbor who commutes for two hours a day for a half percent yearly raise could only dream of.

Consequently, a popular person must always place a high value on his time. Being famous and popular requires you to meet and influence as many people as possible. However, you can't, even if you wish, add hours to the day. It'd be nice to have thirty hours a day to promote yourself and build your fan base while everyone else has twenty four, but it isn't happening!

However, you can do what most people don't: maximize your time. I picked on gamers and those indentured to their jobs, but even if that isn't you, don't think you're getting off easy. The average person watches over four hours of television a day (12)! That number is probably lower now because of the internet, but I'd wager that most people still waste five to six hours a day minimum staring at a screen of some kind. With eight hours of working and commuting added to eight hours of sleep, that leaves one hour of productivity for your own goals on a given weekday! And, I'm sure the weekends aren't any better when tasks like mowing, catching up on sleep, taking the kids places, etc. are factored in.

Another point DeMarco makes in his book that relates to time is how all successful people understand that their success comes from a process, not an event. In other words, behind every celebrity is a process of hard work that led to his current state. Being famous requires lots of hours of networking, cultivating a talent, practicing routines, interacting with others, etc. Even musicians, actors, and sports stars often have years of "lean" times behind them when they worked their butts off for little reward before they hit pay dirt. Make sure that your time is spent becoming successful and popular, and isn't wasted.

So, I want you to start jealously guarding your time right now. Get out a sheet of paper (yes, this is your assignment) and map out your typical day for both Monday through Friday and the weekend. Be honest about what you actually do. If you are a virtual farmer, I promise I won't laugh (too hard).

Now, go through your schedule and find out ways you can cut down on wasting time and start promoting yourself. Trim your video game playing time to an hour a week (or less). Stop sleeping nine hours a night and get busy on something productive like meeting people and creating and maximizing a celebrity brand (see Chapter 35). Or maybe just spend time with family and friends or doing charity. That beats watching a bunch of reality contestants anyway. I know making a schedule seems a little "high school" but you'd be amazed how many adults fritter away their free time with little or no productive gain.

Once you've finished your schedule, resolve to make the most of your time because it's one aspect of life that can't ever be bought back or slowed down. Don't look back on your life when you're old or dying in regret that you spent too many hours playing video games or waiting for cheap hamburgers.

Chapter 33

Open Up (Your Body)

Back in my school teacher days, I had a meeting with my former principal that I'll never forget. She was not a very fun person and she strongly disapproved of the popularity I had with the school's students and their parents. I was presenting a new idea for student learning to my fellow teachers. All my colleagues looked relaxed and open, but my boss had her arms crossed, was leaned back, and was frowning. She had the final say and my idea died right there. Sure, she didn't formally say "no" until weeks later, but she had already told me the answer, not with her mouth, but her body.

Now, don't mourn for me, because getting out of that negative environment was a huge blessing in disguise. What I want you to notice from this story is the body language. I knew, just from a quick glance at body language, that my colleagues were at least open to my thoughts. I also knew that my boss would never give my idea a chance. And this was before any of them even said a word! Your body says just as much, and more, to the people all around you.

If you want to be popular, the first thing you must do is to make sure your body language is open in all social situations. If your body language is closed, all your charming words and witty routines will backfire. The people you're trying to win over will subconsciously notice the incongruity of your words and body language. A popular person should project both confidence and openness to be successful.

Although body language can be incredibly nuanced and complex, generally speaking, if your body is closed, you are viewed as closed; if it's open, you're seen as open. Thus, gestures like crossed legs, crossed arms, covering your neck, shifting away from people while you're talking, etc. are seen as walls to interaction. On the other hand, being spread out, having open arms, open thighs, open lips (a smile), and pointing towards others are seen as welcoming to interaction.

As far as confidence goes, keeping your head high and walking with your chest out slightly are great confident gestures. Look at the way Superman is drawn. He's clearly confident. Another great gesture of confidence is the basketball steeple position. Imagine holding a basketball in your hands around shoulder level. Obviously you shouldn't walk around this way, but if you are giving a presentation or talking to someone you're trying to influence, this position will help you appear more confident.

You may be a little skeptical, but keep in mind these body language cues are typically made and received subconsciously. So, you may be projecting that you're closed and the person you're with will be picking it up too, but neither of you will even be consciously aware of this little interaction! However, it will still impact your opinions of each other. Thus, it's vital to practice being open and confident, even using a mirror if necessary.

There are some special rules that govern body language for romantic type interactions. Although this book isn't concerned necessarily with getting you dates, if you're attractive in the broad sense of the word, you should know how to recognize signs of attraction in other people, so you can respond to them if necessary.

If you're a female, you have it a little easier in reading male body language since guys are pretty straightforward when showing their romantic interest in women. Also, evolution has made women naturally better at reading body language.

A high value male will make eye contact with the girl, approach her, and start talking to her. If he's outgoing, he'll often give her a lot of attention. A low value male will stare at her from across the room for long periods of time. Sometimes, the low value man will get up and talk, but not always. Guys who are medium value will act differently depending on the circumstance. It's usually that simple. Males, in their body language, are typically fairly direct about their intentions, even if it only involves creepily staring at women from across the room.

If you're a man, telling if a woman likes you romantically involves picking up her subtle cues, which is especially difficult since men are naturally less gifted at reading body language anyway. Here are the most common ways a woman shows she's interested. Of course, there are many more. Women readers should examine this list to find techniques to show a guy that they are interested in him. In essence, all of these gestures amount to some form of flirting.

— Playing with her hair, twisting it, etc.

— Showing her exposed neck

— Her feet and/or belly button are pointed toward the guy

— She tells him her name before he asks

— Genuine laughter

— "Preening" herself

— "Cleaning" him - picking lint off of his shirt, adjusting his tie, etc.

— Repeatedly touching him

— Smiling

— Giving him the "once over," i.e. looking up and down your body "checking you out"

— Eye contact

Obviously, my discussion on body language is far from exhaustive. In fact, the topic of body language is an extremely fascinating one that would be to your benefit to master. If you have the time, I would highly advise that you check out the recommended reading section at the end of the book to study body language in more depth. However, the basic rules outlined in this chapter will at least get you started.

Your assignment for this chapter is to go out and observe body language. Before you go, look over the photos at the end of the chapter. Before reading the captions, try to figure out what each person is thinking, and feeling, and how they might react to you.

Go to a coffee shop, mall, club, or somewhere busy. You're here to people watch (although don't make it too obvious or creepy). Observe how people's bodies tell you what they're thinking. Can you find individuals who are happy? What about mad or sad? Who is closed to interaction and who looks fun? Write down your observations. Body language is a fun topic and mastering it will give you a huge social advantage.

It shouldn't be too hard to figure out what everyone is thinking. We are pretty darn good at reading body language naturally. The problems arise when we second guess ourselves. If you're looking for that special someone, keep an eye out for signs of attraction. Oh, and I want you to find an open person and approach him or her. Just go up and say "hello." See what happens.

Thanks to Natalie Howard for being the model for this chapter's photos.

The guy here is confident and having fun. He is standing straight up with his chest out and head up. He likes her, but is barely showing it, which is good. The girl is enjoying his company. She is playing with her hair, showing her wrist, smiling, and pointing her naval to him, which means she likes him in some way.

What happened?? He did something to creep her out, because she is physically moving away from him, her feet are pointed away, and her naval area is pointed away. As a guy, he may be clueless, but all indicators are that he has made a social error. Can he recover? Maybe.

Both people are "body blocking," which means they are uncomfortable or not liking something about the other. This indicates they are closed to interaction with each other. If you are this guy, now is probably not the time to ask her out. To open her up, he should try to get her to gesture with her arms, or else try to build rapport, and put her at ease.

What is she projecting? Her legs and arms are crossed. She is also "hiding" behind the table and drink. She is telegraphing "stay away." If she wanted to meet new people, she should open up. Guys should approach her with caution, unless they are up for a challenge.

Chapter 34

Step Out of The Zone

My first experience with serious romantic rejection was in fourth grade. I had a big crush on a girl named Devon. I didn't know her all that well, so I made an effort to befriend her. After a few weeks of hanging with her, I decided to take it to the next level. I sent her one of those "will you be my boyfriend notes" with the option of checking one: yes, no, or maybe. Sadly, she checked no. But, at least she gave me a reason, which was scribbled underneath her circled no: I think we should just stay friends. I was only nine and had my first taste of the friend zone!

If there is one location that is hell on earth for men (and even many women), it's the "friend zone," where romantic relationships go to die forever, in most cases before they were even born. The friend zone is where a guy finds himself when a woman likes him on an emotional level, but isn't romantically attracted to him. In many cases, the pain is made worse because the woman has no intention of even being his friend. It's simply a way of telling him "you're not a real man, which is what I want; you're like my girlfriends, so be ready for a three in the morning phone call when the guy I'm actually attracted to dumps me." OK, being "friend zoned" may not always tell you that, but it will be something similar.

Whether you're a man or a woman, it's important if you want to be popular to have a diverse group of friends. For example, I take great pride in the fact that I am popular among various groups. I can have fun with gay people just as much as the religious conservatives. It comes with being cool and flexible.

So, having friends of the opposite sex will enrich your life and even help you when it comes time to meet a special someone. Thus, there's nothing wrong with being in the friend zone and there's a lot right about it...so long as that's what you want. But, if you like someone romantically, then you want to avoid the "friend zone" like the plague. So, yes, this is one of those chapters that isn't just devoted to being popular and meeting people, but is focused on dating them.

Since this book is primarily aimed at creating popular men, I'm going to start with helpful tips to allow men to stay out of the friend zone. I'm going to give techniques to execute one of the most tricky and daring exploits as well: escaping the friend zone once you're already there. Afterward, as a benefit to my female readers, I'll also talk about ways women can exit the friend zone with men.

Before I lay out my tips to avoid the friend zone, it's helpful to remember what women value in a man they want to date: power, leadership, strength, and other traits that show her he is high value. Most women want a man who can provide for them and protect them in some way. This is not saying a woman is helpless and needs a man. Even an independent minded woman still wants someone who can make her feel secure and loved. Women also like a man who can give a little edge to their lives, someone who is exciting and maybe even a little mysterious.

It's also helpful to remember what a woman looks for in her female friends. She wants girlfriends who are emotionally available, which is why women are often accused of being gossips. It's not that they're spreading rumors, but they typically just like to talk about their days, their needs, etc. Men do this kind of venting too, but women have actually evolved to talk more (13). While true, you may not want to point out this fact in the midst of a fight with your mom or girlfriend.

To avoid the friend zone, you have to make the right first impression. From the start, you must telegraph to her that you are boyfriend material, not friend material. This sounds harsh, but once you genuinely become her friend, you are viewed just like her girlfriends. Would you date your guy friends (if you're straight)? I highly doubt it. Well, she will view you the same way once you're in the friend zone. You're her friend; nothing more. And, most times, she will size you up and decide whether you're boyfriend material almost immediately.

To demonstrate you are boyfriend quality, you have to avoid appearing low value. You have to push her evolutionarily programmed attraction buttons. Project your status as a provider and protector as much as possible by your body language (see Chapter 33) and in the way you speak and act. Be a real man around her and not one of her girlfriends. Be confident and assertive, but not too cocky. Have an edge, but don't be a jerk. Let her think you're the most popular guy in the place, which, if you're following this book, you should be.

Second, you have to make her desire you. Women typically find nice, butt-kissing guys boring (see Chapter 18 to review how to be more assertive) and unattractive. Sure, they'll take your compliments and the drink you bought them, but they won't be dating you. You'll have to make sure that she wants you far more than you want her (even if this is untrue).

When you're around her, act detached (see Chapter 15). Don't buy her a drink (in fact, if she asks you to buy her one, playfully tell her she should buy you one!). Avoid too many compliments and instead tease her gently. It sounds counter-intuitive, but it actually gets women to like you. If you take her out to dinner, unless you're dating, split the bill or only pay for little things like coffee. Oh, and when you text her, delay a little bit. Never appear attached or desperate.

Finally, man up and move the relationship in a more romantic direction. If you've been following my previous advice, then she doesn't yet view you as one of her girlfriends. However, she may not be fully sexually attracted to you either. You're more in the neutral zone. That's when you step up the game. You can do this by more actively flirting with her and even being more direct about your romantic intentions.

I know some of this advice sounds harsh and isn't politically correct. However, the dating game can be harsh and women play it just as much as men. When a woman gets a free dinner from a guy she has no intention of dating, it's not nice either. I just want you to be a step ahead and come out on top. Also, at least with these methods, you're being honest with yourself and the girl. I don't know how many guys befriend women for the sole purpose of trying to date them. They have no intention of even being their friend. That is unhealthy for both sides and often leads to an undoing of the friendship as both sides become frustrated: him with the lack of romance and her with the gradual revelation of his ulterior motives

If you are stuck in the friend zone, getting out can be tough. However, it can be done if you really want to. But, I would argue that if you're in the friend zone with a girl already, just stay there and enjoy the friendship. There are way too many available women out there. Still, if you really want to leave the friend zone with a special girl, you'll have to gradually show her that you're boyfriend material. This means increasing your value by getting a better job, moving into positions of power or leadership, getting fitter, etc. It also means you'll have to stop sucking up to her (if you do this). You also will probably need to be scarce for a while so she can "re-discover" your new, high value self. Remember, familiarity breeds contempt.

Now I want to talk to the ladies who are friend zoned with men they are attracted to. First, I want to address a common scenario: where you are in the friend zone, but the guy actually wants a romantic relationship. Many men are shy and lack confidence when it comes to taking the relationship to the next level. In this case, he may just need some extra clues or hints that you like him, so he feels confident that you won't reject him if he asks you out on a date. You may even want to be direct and ask him his feelings about you. Or you can ramp up the flirting extra hard.

If you truly are in the friend zone and you know the guy doesn't like you, then you'll have to take similar advice that I gave the men: make yourself more attractive. This typically means you'll need to become more physically appealing to him. Sometimes women act less feminine around their male friends. However, being "one of the guys" isn't typically good for romance. So, start wearing makeup around him, do your hair, and generally try to make yourself more attractive. It may take a while, but eventually he'll notice. This same advice applies if you are out meeting new people. Look your best when you're going out to attract men romantically. It will prevent you from being friend zoned in the first place.

Although, when you go out, you likely won't be asked to circle "yes," "no," or "maybe" on a note from a stranger, with these tips, you will, at the very least be more likely to get a "yes" or a "maybe" (which you will turn into a "yes"). Unless you're looking for friendship, I hope these techniques will help you take a vacation from the friend zone...permanently.

Your assignment is to identify girls (or guys for our female readers) in your life who may have friend zoned you over the years. List their names, then give the reasons why you think you ended up as a friend instead a romantic partner. Then, identify a few ways you think you could've avoided the friend zone with these individuals. Keep these good tips in mind when you approach romantic relationships in the future. A few of the upcoming chapters will make sure that you have plenty of those as well.

CHAPTER 35

BUILDING A BRAND

My first year of teaching, I went in with a great attitude. I wanted to be popular, admired, and effective. The first year I wore a cool outfit during our school's Halloween costume day. The students voted on a faculty winner and I expected to be the one. However, I lost to another teacher who wore a rainbow colored wig! That's it! I knew he only won because he was popular. I realize now that I, as a new teacher, was still being evaluated by the students to see if I was going to be a cool and beloved teacher. Adam, on the other hand, had already established himself as a very popular teacher. He had an image. He had a brand.

If you are an adult who is going to be popular, you need to be very aware of your image and even work to build up that image. Call it a "celebrity brand" if you like, but regardless of the name, it's important. For those of you who have no dreams of bigger celebrity, you still need to pay attention.

First, because we live in a very invasive age, everything we do has the potential to be used against us. This means that rumors, misunderstandings, and even actual facts, if in the wrong hands, can deal a blow to not only your aspirations of popularity, but also your career, family, etc. Just check the news to see how many times a dumb tweet, a stupid Facebook photo, or an unscripted comment has seriously damaged someone's reputation, whether previously famous or not.

Second, many people in our lives want to define us in some fashion. They often do so because it gives them power and control in relationships. Sadly, not all of these definitions are in our best interests. Even family, friends, co-workers, and acquaintances will try to tell us who we are. It's not always easy to break out of those expectations. Creating a careful public image is a good way to control your identity.

Now that we've discussed the bad news, now it's time to focus on the positive side. The internet also allows for quick branding or re-branding as well. With social media and easy creation of websites, reputations can be quickly changed, modified, or even created out of thin air.

Your first step will be to create a unique image. Notice the word unique. If your brand is like everyone else's, then you offer nothing to other people. Why would they admire a clone when the original is better anyway? So, think about what is unique about your traits, talents, and overall personality. It may be helpful to list these (see practice assignment). Then, figure out what aspect you'd like to focus on.

If you are still working on improving yourself, then build your brand around the traits outlined in your avatar (see Chapter 6). However, make sure that you continue to work towards your success goals because your image has to be legitimate or you'll have no credibility.

When you decide what you want your brand to be, you'll have to start letting those traits guide your public life. This includes when you're working, in your home life, on your websites, and on social media. For example, if you decide that being funny is a part of your image, then you need to let your humor shine through wherever you go. This means you are funny at work, with your family, in your social life, with your social media presence, and anywhere else.

After you've established the brand, you need to make sure you live it consistently. An image can be created, but it won't last long unless it's consistent and congruent. This is especially true if you're trying to reinvent yourself after being unpopular. If a lot of people know the old you, it may take a little bit of time for the new you to sink in with them.

It's very important to publicly live your image consistently because otherwise it negates the point of establishing one to begin with. Let's say you decide you want a cool, laid back image. If you're constantly creating drama on Facebook or at work, then your image isn't really being maintained. In fact, you may actually be creating another image: that of a hypocrite who says one thing, then goes and does the exact opposite. Creating the image is the easy part; maintaining it is more difficult.

Be patient when it comes to your brand. If you research famous celebrities, you'll notice that they built up their images over time. Don't try to rush it or get impatient. When I was a teacher, it took at least a year for me to build up my popularity level to become known as the "popular teacher" among the students. Rightfully, they waited to see if my long-term actions corresponded to the image I tried to project from the beginning. The same will be true of you.

You may need to change your image at points too. If you do, then remember to do it gradually or people will think you're fake. I knew a girl who changed interests every time she got a new boyfriend. One week she was a cowgirl and the next week she was a gangster. She had a reputation as a follower who changed on a whim. The moral is: if you need to reinvent yourself, do it gradually.

Once your brand is established long term, then popularity actually becomes a lot easier. My first year of teaching I had to work hard to establish my "brand" of teaching, which differed from everyone else's. And, with teens, there was little margin for error! However, once I succeeded and my image was established, then my reputation preceded me. Incoming students heard about me, so I had to work less to win them over. I was the one winning contests solely based on my popularity, while newer teachers had to compete with me.

As much as I harp on consistency, you don't have to live up to your image all of the time. That would be way too exhausting. Even famous people take a break from their image. I highly doubt Gene Simmons wears the makeup and sticks out his tongue at home. Then again, it's hard to tell. It may be helpful to pick places where you want to be "on" like social media, out at clubs, etc. and schedule time to be "off" at others.

For your assignment, I'd like you to create your image/brand. List eight to ten traits or talents that you want to comprise your public image. You can start by revisiting the traits you outlined for your avatar in Chapter 6. You may also want to think of the various characteristics your favorite celebrities possess. Some examples could be: musically talented, laid back, funny, etc. When you've finished, write out places where you're going to publicly promote those traits. Some examples may be work, school, Facebook, etc.

The next three chapters explain the three part process of meeting new people (the approach, building rapport, and the close). Right now, you should have the "theory" of being popular down as well as some real world practice. Now you're moving from practice to the game itself.

CHAPTER 36

MASTER THE APPROACH

She was beautiful, with her long, thick brown hair, green eyes, and easy smile. She had a killer body too, which was evident when she sat down to enjoy her coffee each morning during winter quarter of my junior year at Ohio University. My memory of her is still fairly vivid, but I don't know her name. It's not because I'm getting older; I never knew it to begin with. You see, as much as I liked this girl and desperately wanted to talk to her, I couldn't. My brain, so useful during my classes, had stopped me cold. Like many other men, I had trouble approaching strangers, especially beautiful ladies.

Men and women are brain wired to interact with each other in different ways. Although this book is primarily aimed at men, I recognize that it has valuable tips for female readers too (and you might be one). So, I've included a section for both men and women in this chapter. I highly recommend that, whatever your sex, you read the entire chapter. The approach, rapport building, and the close really are the human mating game, so it's vital to understand the role of the opposite sex in that ritual too.

For men:

Back in the earliest days of humanity, the social scene wasn't as innocuous as it is today. In the tribal era, the time of polygamy, the tribe's chieftain and his relatives typically pursued the best women and created a harem for themselves. They also picked the best and strongest men to be their peers and warriors. These were the Alpha Males. The lesser men, the betas, were frequently forced to pursue the leftovers. Many were lucky to have any friends and received no woman at all. In addition, the social hierarchy in the village was determined by who could kick the most butt in any given population.

You can probably guess that social interaction was much more difficult and dangerous in the past. If you approached a female, there was a good chance she was taken by an Alpha Male, either as a wife or daughter. In that case, there was also a good chance you would literally be killed if you made a misstep (unless you were tough enough to resist)! The same was also true for interacting with other men. If you weren't tough enough to fight and hunt with the big guys, you would likely get your butt whipped for even trying.

Fast forward to modern times. Today, at least in the United States, it's very unlikely that you will be killed for approaching a woman at a bar, or asked to fight another man for the right to attend a networking meeting. However, the brain still feels like if you approach another person and fail, you very well might die. For example, think about the best looking girl you know. Now, think about asking her out. How do you feel? If you're a typical male, you probably feel at least a little nervous, if not scared out of your mind.

This feeling is called "approach anxiety" and it's hard wired into the male brain. Your brain is trying to protect your sorry ass and doesn't realize it's actually hindering your success with others, whether it's for business, romance, or friendship. I haven't yet met any man who has gotten rid of approach anxiety completely, by which I mean the initial feeling you get when thinking of approaching a woman or a high value man. However, approach anxiety can be controlled. Celebrities and popular men do it all the time.

The first way to combat approach anxiety is to remember that approaching someone won't kill you. You're not going to undo hundreds of thousands of years of evolution in a week, but the rational side of your brain can keep the older parts in check. Each time you are ready to approach a man or woman, take charge of your brain. Acknowledge that the more primitive part of your brain is trying to sabotage you and then remind yourself that you will not die. There is no death by rejection. Your rational side took millions of years to evolve, so take advantage of it! This method is useful for all settings, and when dealing with both sexes.

The second method is to have a "shoot down set." This technique is for picking up women in a club or other social setting and shouldn't be used with guys at all, or for women in business type settings. As soon as you enter a club or other venue where women are looking to meet men, approach a group of girls and ask them to shoot you down (meaning insult you).

Using humor is perhaps the best way to do this (say something like "my self-esteem is just too high tonight. I really need you to shoot me down"). If they comply, you will have been put down and guess what? You survived! This method really is helpful to banish anxiety for the rest of the night. The irrational part of your brain (the stem) loses its control because your rational brain knows you're still alive. You can relax. Also, I've found that very few women will actually shoot you down (and if they do, it's because you asked them to!). You may even make new friends or romantic partners from this activity. I want to give a special shout out to Joshua Wagner for coming up with this great idea.

Third, approach anxiety can be countered by mastering the other techniques in this book like flexibility, humor, open body language, etc. The more confident, high value, and detached you become, the less approach anxiety rules your life. Basically, as you become more popular and famous, it gets easier. Do you think someone like George Clooney is hampered by approach anxiety? I highly doubt it.

Finally, the key to destroying approach anxiety is to approach others often. The more you do it, the more you'll realize that approaching new people won't kill you and you'll even discover it can actually be pretty fun. After all, as a beloved and popular guy, your approach leads to cool outcomes like getting attention, meeting new people, and making fans. That's a pretty good deal, even if your irritating, but essential, brain stem doesn't appreciate it. However, as I mentioned, it is nearly impossible to *eliminate* approach anxiety. Acknowledge it and deal with it when it rears its head.

For women:

When evolution established the mating ritual, it gave females a more passive role. This may sound sexist, but it simply fits with the facts. Women are typically physically weaker, and they had to defer to the more physically powerful men in the community. So, instead of approaching the men and getting their way through power and confidence, they had to be approached and use other techniques to either accept or reject a man.

However, I'm not implying women are the weaker partners in the complex approach ritual. To the contrary, female brains developed to clearly show their availability or lack of it. So, if you have mastered the crossed arms, eye roll, and icy stare, you are using your gift from evolution to ward off loser guys.

However, in the modern world, there are two methods women

need to take when "approaching" men. First, and this applies to the clubs, bars, festivals, etc. where men are actively trying to approach you, you simply have to be available. You do this through being open, friendly, and relaxed. I covered this in the body language section (see Chapter 33). If you're having trouble being open, review that information. In these types of social situations, nature has given guys the hard work of approaching you and then dealing with your verbal and non-verbal clues. If you are interested in a man, you project openness; if you are not interested, you must project unavailability.

However, be aware that if you want to be popular, it never hurts to project availability to everyone, at least in the general, non-sexual sense. Even if the guy is a loser, have a conversation, maybe get a free drink, and move on. If you're friendly, you may have at minimum found a friend, a networking contact, or someone who at least thinks you're cool.

The second approach method applies when you are in other social settings, such as networking situations. Here it is perfectly acceptable to approach others and you shouldn't wait for a person to come to you. If you get nervous and develop approach anxiety, read my tips for overcoming it in the "for men" section of this chapter.

However, here's a word of advice when approaching others at business events. If you are dealing with a man, even in a non-sexual situation, many of the same dynamics apply to the advice I gave for the clubs, bars, etc. It's just the way nature has wired men to deal with the opposite sex. So, don't be surprised if you find yourself being a little more passive and even flirtatious. It's not going to hurt you since, as a woman, you have many, many subtle tricks at your disposal to win over guys, even the more dominant ones. Use those to your advantage.

For everyone:

In the end, the best advice for both sexes is to relax and have a good time. Remember, approaching others isn't going to kill you. In fact, think about all of the amazing people out there whom you'd love to meet. If you don't approach them and they don't approach you, then you'll never connect with them.

The risk of approach seems like it's a big one since rejection can be hard to take. However, in reality, being rejected by a total stranger you'll likely never see again is a small risk. But, if you meet a new best friend, a great networking connection, or even a future spouse, that is a great reward indeed. Basically, you can approach others knowing that the risk is pretty small and the potential reward could be life-changing.

Your assignment is to go out tonight and approach five random people. However, let me give you a word of advice: it's best to go somewhere where people are anticipating an approach, at least if this is your first time. I'd recommend a social event, club, or busy coffee shop or mall. Remember to use your routines. Try to keep the conversation going, but at this point don't stress too much about follow up. Just approach five people. If you're a man and in a bar, try a shoot down set. It'll make the other approaches a piece of cake.

CHAPTER 37

BUILD SOME RAPPORT

Back in my teaching days, we would frequently have meetings where we would discuss so-called difficult students. I always found those a waste of time because I didn't really consider any students to be difficult. In fact, a lot of the students who created trouble for other teachers absolutely loved me. One day, in the teacher's lounge, a colleague was asking how I'd managed to reach a particularly headstrong and angry student, so he could do the same. He looked shocked when I gave such a simple, non-academic answer: I just listened to the kid.

As a teacher, I had many assets that made me popular, such as my sense of humor and the ease at which I related to other people. Yet, perhaps the biggest secret of my success is that, at the start of every year, I made an effort to get to know every student personally in some way. I actually talked to them and valued their opinions. It sounds very mundane, but in education, what I did was extremely radical: I built genuine rapport with my teenage students and actually liked them. Building rapport, or developing a relationship with another person, is essential to become popular and create lasting relationships.

While "the approach" may be the most difficult to get started due to anxiety, once introduced, two strangers can usually get along well enough in the beginning. After all, being witty, throwing out a few jokes, or discussing the weather for several minutes is pretty easy. Building rapport, which involves a lot of listening and paying attention, is actually a little harder. However, if you took the advice on mindfulness and paying attention to heart (see Chapters 12 and 23), then rapport building isn't going to be that tough for you.

It may be helpful to think of rapport building as getting on the same wavelength with someone else. Have you ever heard someone say "I like his vibe?" A vibe is a vibration or wave. If you hear a vibration, it's possible to mimic it with your voice or another instrument. By doing this, you would be "on the same wavelength." Look at rapport building the same way. The person you've approached is a unique individual you want to get to know better. Find out his or her "vibe" and get in tune with it. That's all I did with my students really. I listened to them and then did my best to get in tune with their academic, emotional, developmental needs.

Obviously, rapport building is a two way street. But, as a future celebrity, you will have to take the lead and probably even do most of the work. This is especially true if you are a man or you've approached someone shy. Just remember that the more rapport you build and the more comfortable the person becomes, the more your two "wavelengths" will converge. If it sounds tough, don't worry because I have some helpful advice to achieve this. The first three tips come from psychologist and founder of Neuro-Linguistic Programming (NLP) Richard Bandler. I'd highly recommend any of his books to all of my readers (see Sources/Recommended Reading).

The first tip is called behavioral mirroring. As the name implies, you will mirror another person's behavior. You can adjust the pitch of your voice, your position, tone, breathing, speed of talking, posture, movement, etc. to match the other person's. If they put their arms on the table or cross their legs, you would do the same. Make sure you're subtle, otherwise it may look weird or appear as if you are mocking them. Mirroring breathing seems to be particularly effective, but also subtle enough that the conscious mind does not notice it.

Another good tip is to use symbolic mirroring. This is taking someone else's symbols and using them. An example would be if you want to convince a liberal audience of a conservative point, speak to them using the language of a liberal. If you want to find success with people in a country bar, you could wear western clothes. Listen carefully for cues when you first meet people. They often give away their symbolic preferences liberally in conversation. For example, someone may tell you when discussing their job situation, "I finally see the light at the end of the tunnel." Later in the conversation, when it's your turn, you could use light/tunnel language for explaining your own success. Be creative on this one, but again don't appear to be satirizing or mocking the people you're trying to win over.

Third, you should try pacing and matching. This is different than mirroring and involves integrating parts of a person's personality, speech, and mannerisms into your own way of communicating. This could involve using another person's vocabulary (you know, like, talking like a teen to reach a teenager), or their representative system (e.g. if they are primarily auditory, use phrases such as "I hear you;" if they are primarily visual, say "I see that," etc.). You may even start to do this naturally as the conversation continues. It's amazing how much mirroring occurs naturally in human interaction.

Another easy way to build rapport is to simply listen. Obviously, there are many cases where you want to talk a lot, like when you approach people in a busy place and want to show them your high value. However, to build rapport, you'll have to stop and actually listen at some point. With my students I combined a teaching style that was entertaining with one on one time where I could find out the teen's interests and needs. You should also have a good mix of showing your personal charm and taking time to actually listen. Extroverted people need to remember this especially because if one person dominates the conversation, it'll get tiresome quickly for the "spectator."

After you have listened, you should have gathered some

information about the other person. Next, use this information to build more rapport. People usually volunteer enough information about themselves for you to find some common interests or at least potential topics of conversation. If the person brought up getting back from the gym, you can use that as a conversation topic later, by asking them something about their work-out habits, and then sharing yours. One time David's wife was shopping and started talking to another woman about an item they were both buying. It turns out they knew a lot of people in common from the woman's hometown ninety miles away.

Finally, you should assume rapport. In other words, act like you've already built rapport with the person you've approached. This belief will affect your own body language and attitude, taking some stress from the situation. After all, you wouldn't have any trouble talking to your friends. Assuming rapport may even "trick" the person you've met into thinking you already know them. I've done this on many occasions to great effect. I walk up to strangers and say something like, "Hey, long time no see! How have you been?" In most cases they'll smile and talk to me and only later ask, "How do I know you exactly?" When I say that they don't, everyone typically has a good laugh. In some cases, I've actually made new friends this way. But, by assuming rapport, I achieved my primary goal of getting to know them. In other words, I actually built rapport by assuming it!

While I haven't divided this chapter into male and female sections, I was tempted. I think it's worth saying that when men and women are interacting with each other, building rapport is a little more complicated. Once again, it's an issue of brain wiring and the different ways the sexes process information.

If you are a woman talking to a man, realize that men often don't think in emotional terms. Men are brain wired to focus more on hard facts. It's why the engineer and accountant professions are overwhelmingly male. It also explains why women rarely play fantasy football or take an interest in sports statistics. If you're a woman talking to a man, you may want to build rapport by playing down the emotional aspects of the conversation and focus instead on the facts, details, objective observations, etc. Most men will certainly be more engaged in such an exchange.

If you are a man talking to a woman, realize that women typically focus on emotions, in other words, how they feel about a specific topic. Let's look at an example from sports. My wife goes to football games with me sometimes. She enjoys being in the crowd of people, talking to people she knows, and discussing the patterns on the cheerleading outfits. She also likes how the game is fast-paced and interesting. However, she doesn't seem to care at all about the rules of the game or my attempts to explain them. For her, it is about the emotional experience.

Instead of relying on facts and objective observations, men should try to speak to women using what John Alexander, author of <u>How to Be an Alpha Male</u>, calls emotionally relevant language. This means framing your conversations in terms of your reactions to experiences. Let me give you an example. You drive to meet a girl for coffee. Rather than talking about the details of the trip, the specific business deals you made that day, and other facts, explain how you experienced your day and the trip over. You might say, "I saw the coolest thing on the way over" or "I felt really intrigued by something a client said this morning." You've explained your day, but in a way that focuses on experience and emotions.

However, you'll want to avoid being too emotional. Emotionalism comes across to a woman as needy, girly, and low value. An example of emotionalism from the above story would be saying "I'm so angry at my partner's secretary that I could just punch something." Although it is emotional and is speaking from experience, it just isn't the behavior of a high value man.

Of course, these rules for building rapport with men and women are just general guidelines. There will always be men and women who deviate from these stereotypes, so don't get too comfortable with the assumptions. Remember, whatever the circumstance, you will adapt (Chapter 9)!

Your assignment for this chapter is to go out and actually build rapport. I know it sounds silly, but try it with someone you know at first. It's low pressure, so you can try the techniques without looking silly or condescending, and you'll probably get to know the person a lot better. You'd be amazed how little rapport often exists between friends and acquaintances. After you test your mettle with some family members or friends, I want you to go out in the field and try it with total strangers. Build rapport with at least two people.

CHAPTER 38

CLOSE THE DEAL

When I was five, what I really wanted for Christmas was a Wonder Woman action figure (I won't use the word doll). Don't judge me too harshly; I had a huge crush on Lynda Carter who played Wonder Woman on the old television show. I had it all figured out: I would ask Santa when he made his yearly appearance at the local church's Christmas concert. I got up the courage to sit on Santa's lap, made some small talk with him, and asked for a side gift or two. However, when it came time to ask for Wonder Woman, I clammed up. Instead, I asked for a puzzle.

You may be master of the approach and rapport building, but if you can't make the close, then you're pretty much out of luck. It's like finding a great dish on a menu in a fancy restaurant, but being too scared to order it. Failing to make the close will, in social situations, leave you pretty lonely. Many men especially have missed out on relationships with beautiful women (maybe even wonder women) because they were too scared to get their contact information.

There are a variety of psychological reasons why it's hard to make the close. I think for many people, it comes down to a simple lack of confidence: they fear being rejected. It feels pretty bad when you've gotten to know someone and you ask for his or her number, only to be shot down after all that effort. I also think that talking to someone on a casual basis requires little personal risk. But, actually opening yourself up for continual connection with another human being can be scary, especially if you've had bad or disappointing relationships in the past.

Whether you fear the close or not, if you don't make it, you'll miss out on many opportunities since "closing" allows you to be more intimately connected with others. They could be new friends, potential mates, or valuable networking partners that can take your quest for fame and success to a whole new level. Entertaining the masses in one off approaches is great, but you still need those deeper, lasting connections too. Here are my guidelines for successfully making the close.

The first is to simply give someone your contact information, like through that old standby, a business card. In many cases, this is a low stress option. You simply say, "I've really enjoyed talking with you, maybe we should try this again sometime" and give them your card.

Adding a bit of humor and making yourself look good may be helpful too. This could be as easy as saying, "Since I know you had such a good time talking to me, here's my card." Say this with a smile or the person will think you're arrogant. Giving your new connections a business card is low stress, but it has a couple of disadvantages. First, if it's not the right social environment, giving a business card can be dorky. Also, you must rely on the other person to follow-up, which may never happen. The ideal situation is to get them to give you their information so you control how the follow-up is done. Remember, you always want to be in charge.

I've found another easy way to close with someone is through social media. When you're done with the conversation, you can suggest you both be friends on Facebook, connect on LinkedIn, follow each other on Twitter, etc. If you don't want to be direct (and sometimes indirect is better), say something like "we have a lot in common, so maybe we should stay connected on Facebook." People are often more comfortable adding friends on social media than giving out their number, because Facebook, Twitter, and other sites offer more options for privacy. In addition, with smart phones, it's possible to add and/or confirm the person right there so you leave the encounter certain of having made the close.

If you want to get someone's number, I recommend creating a need for the person you're talking with to contact you. For example, if I meet someone I like and want to get to know better, I'll typically bring up my business. I'm always looking for contributors, graphic designers, extras in photos, etc. and I will sometimes bring this up (casually and indirectly, so people aren't scared off). Sometimes those I'm talking to will express interest in meeting my business needs (and making a few bucks in the process), so they want to connect with me and even suggest it. This is because if people think there is a benefit for them, they will happily give you their number, Facebook information, or anything else really. Of course, if you're high value, the benefit could simply be from knowing you and joining your social circle.

The easiest way to practice making closes is to go to networking events. Eager people come to these for the sole purpose of giving and getting contact information, so you won't have to worry about annoying anyone or getting rejected. Approaching and closing are what you do there. Plus, those events can be fun since they're often centered around social activities. Check the internet to see if there's a networking group in your area and try to get involved in their activities. It will be a great way to practice meeting people and making the close. It also may help you get a better job, build your business, or just find someone to hang out with on weekends.

There are a few guidelines to remember when making the close. Unless it's clearly business, you'll have to build some comfort and rapport with the person first. Simply going up to another person, saying a few lines, and asking for a number won't usually work. Also, in social settings, men are expected to make the close with women. Except in extreme cases, women aren't likely to volunteer their information unless they really, really like the guy. Men, it's your job!

It's best to keep the close process simple. You should get the number or other contact information before the interaction is over. Going back to ask for it later, having someone else get it for you, looking the person up on Facebook when you get home, or any indirect, late, or Rube Goldberg methods (look him up) should be avoided. They all make you look timid and lacking in confidence. A confident, popular man will have no trouble asking for someone's number or other contact info, and will do it before the conversation is over.

Also, if you fail to get any contact information, don't feel bad. It's not always a reflection on the job you did or your value. Maybe the person you talked to has a jealous boyfriend and giving out her number would cause her lots of problems. Some people are also just naturally private or loners too. Having said that, most people are more than happy to make new connections, especially if they think connecting with you has some benefit for them.

Also, after you've made the close, don't appear over eager. I see this mistake all the time with men. Guys will get a girl's number and text her before either of them even leaves the club! Wait a couple of days to follow up. If your contact is time sensitive, then at least delay twenty-four hours. You want the person to think you're high value, which means you are busy and have other people and opportunities taking up your time. Plus, making the person you're contacting with sweat a little isn't so bad. Let her be desperate for your time and attention, not the other way around.

Your practice assignment is to go out to a club or other popular, social themed venue or event on a Friday or Saturday night and practice all three aspects of meeting someone new: approaching, building rapport, and closing. Try not to leave without getting a new contact. Giving your business card is acceptable, but a phone number or friend on Facebook is preferable.

CHAPTER 39

GO OUT AND BLESS OTHERS

To be honest, I wasn't sure where to put this chapter. I almost made it the first chapter, but after some thought, I felt it belonged at the end, as a reminder of what being popular is really all about. If you've been paying attention, you've noticed that I've used the word "bless" a lot throughout the entire book. This is intentional and not an effort to secretly inject religious values into the book.

The word "bless" comes from a Germanic word that means "to make sacred through sacrifice." If you're rolling your eyes right now, bear with me! This actually has a lot to do with being popular.

As I've said countless times, people become celebrities for one reason: they give others what they need. It can be entertainment, a purpose, a product, or whatever. Being a celebrity takes hard work and a huge time commitment. Do you think U2's million selling albums make themselves? Imagine for a minute the thousands of hours of practice, playing in dive bars, and other sacrifices each member of the band made before they became one of the biggest acts in the world. Each and every genuinely popular person puts in similar hard work. Even the cast of Jersey Shore, as annoying as they may be, aren't sitting on their butts playing video games all day.

When you go out in the world and share your wit, humor, openness, and high value, you are giving of yourself. If done correctly, you will leave people better off than before they met you. It may be in the form of more laughter, a break from a lousy job, or a valuable friendship. You go out among the population and create mini "peak moments" in people's days and they will love you for it and want to be around you. Voila! Popularity. These may not be sacred moments in the religious sense of the word, but I think the image still fits. You've made someone's day, maybe even life, better and more worth living. That's sacredness in my book (at least this one).

But, as you know, the celebrity lifestyle isn't all about sacrifice. Most people, when you give of yourself to them, will happily give in return. Popular bands give great music and their fans give back in the form of buying their albums and attending their concerts. Famous athletes give their bodies and their energy to entertain fans who then reward them by paying for tickets and buying their merchandise. You may not become a Hollywood millionaire, but the people you touch on a daily basis will almost always happily give back to you in whatever way they can.

As a teacher, I gave my time, energy, and much more on a daily basis to my students. I didn't just show up and teach, but gave of myself. As a result, I was popular and loved throughout the entire school. When the administration sought to get rid of me, the students rose up in mass protest. So did many of their parents. It was because I had sacrificed of myself to make the lives of their children more meaningful. Even though the unpopular administration refused to relent, the people in the school that mattered most, the students and their parents, had my back.

This is a perfect example of "making sacred through sacrifice" and getting a blessing in return. I could've been like the majority of teachers who show up for a job, throw up a few boring notes on the board, and high tail it out of there at 3:30pm. Sure, there were times when I wanted to do just that. But, instead, I gave of myself and blessed my students and their families. As a result of my blessing them, they turned around and blessed me in any way they could, whether it was the student sit in they organized or parents passing along networking opportunities.

My experience as a teacher wasn't unique. I act like a celebrity everywhere I go, so I bless others everywhere I go. And, those people, in turn, bless me. Why would anyone not want to be popular when this is what it's really all about? And, if you truly focus on blessing others, you will be popular. And you will be blessed in return. This I guarantee.

I haven't focused much on being a celebrity in the Hollywood sense, but I want to say a few words about it now. Hollywood celebrities, in spite of their foibles and outright foolishness, still bless millions of people. If you can find a way to bless millions of people, then you too will be rich and famous.

So, start small by finding popularity in your own environment, then work your way up to bigger things. Think of a great idea or find another way to bless millions or even billions of people. That is the path to becoming a bigger, more famous celebrity. Just don't lose sight of the most important thing: as a popular, successful guy (or lady), you meet the needs of other people and make their lives better. That is true whether you are beloved by twenty people in your small Kansas town or millions throughout the world.

CONCLUSION

WRAPPING IT ALL UP

I hope you found this book entertaining and helpful. Even more, I hope it has changed your life. I want to reiterate that achieving celebrity status involves a lot of effort (but fun effort), constant practice, and the willingness to adapt under some socially difficult situations. Basically, just reading this book alone won't make you more popular. Going out and practicing what you've learned – and making it a habit – will.

My goal is that you actually become really, really popular. I hope that a few months from now, you are popular, beloved, and a celebrity wherever you find yourself, whether it's in college, at your job, or in your knitting circle. I'm not just saying this because you've bought my book and are, in a sense, my student. Believe it or not, I sincerely think that the world needs more popular people, not fewer. I've seen how happy other people become when my friends and I interact with them. I've witnessed how lives are changed by simply paying attention. I've also noticed how the world is a better place when everyone gives, gets, then gives back in a cycle of blessing others.

Not only that, but I can also tell you from personal experience that being popular is fun as hell. You meet some awesome people, get attention whenever you want it, and never have to be bored. Shoot, I know that if I'm having a boring day, I can go anywhere I want and light up the room. Not only that, but as much as I've given, I've gotten more back than I can even express in the form of gifts, opportunities, and above all, friendships. The friendships I've formed in the last few years are my favorite part of being popular.

If you still haven't quite mastered the material in this book or just want a helping hand in setting and achieving your goals, we will help you out. At our websites The Popular Man (thepopularman.com), The Popular Teen (thepopularteen.com) and Popular Teacher (popularteacher.com), we strive to provide you with the best tools possible for you to become successful and unstoppable.

Becoming popular is just the beginning. We have many techniques to help people become excellent in whatever they do. We also have other books available in addition to this one. Please visit our websites and sign up for our newsletters, so you can receive regular updates with helpful tips and ideas for becoming your best self.

So, close your e-reader or put down the book and get out there and apply what you've learned! Go out and have fun meeting people and sharing with them the awesome power of *you*!

FREQUENTLY ASKED QUESTIONS

AND OUR ANSWERS

1. Who are you anyway? Are you even famous?

I'm Jonathan Bennett, writing with my brother David...duh. I don't claim to be world famous, just popular and well-known in all my environments. Remember that the odds of being world famous are tiny. I'm helping you achieve a very realistic and attainable goal: popularity wherever you are right now – which is exactly what I've done in my own life.

2. I'm ugly. I can't be popular. Right?

See Chapter 16. But, to reiterate, you don't have to be great-looking to be popular. You just have to be fun, exciting, and high value. And give people something they need. But, being good-looking never hurts.

3. Why do you talk so much about starting a business? It's not even realistic for everyone.

I talk a lot about starting a business for two reasons. First, I've done it myself and love it. The second is because I believe strongly that being your own boss is the best way to go. Not only does it increase your earning potential and personal freedom, it is incredibly attractive to most people.

And yes, it is realistic. With the internet, there are few barriers stopping even the average person from pursuing some kind of entrepreneurial goal. I'd highly recommend reading Millionaire Fastlane and Effortless Entrepreneur to get started. Plus, if you're a dude, you get an added benefit to being a business owner: chicks love rich, independent men.

4. I wasn't popular in high school. Isn't it too late?

The most popular guy at my high school works a very average job and the most popular girl is a homemaker. Nothing against either of these people, because I'm sure they're still charming and popular, but your status in high school or any past lack of popularity is not an indicator of anything in the present. Even if you were the champ at "Magic the Gathering" back in the 90's you can re-invent yourself. And your card playing secret is safe with me.

5. Does this book really work? Is it really this easy?

Yes and maybe. The book does work. Not only did I follow the techniques outlined here to revamp my life and become popular, but these same principles have helped friends and clients as well. However, the question of "being easy" is different. If you can follow the principles in this book, then it's actually pretty easy to get people to like you. However, if you've learned bad patterns and habits, then following the principles each day may be kind of hard. But, the techniques in the book do work. Keep trying and don't give up.

6. Do these techniques work on everyone? The girl I work with just rolled her eyes at me.

They do for the vast majority. Human nature is pretty straightforward and predictable, and these tips will be effective with most people. However, they're not going to work for absolutely every person you encounter. The personalities of people out there are simply too diverse. Of course, you'll find people who won't like you. But for every person you meet like this, you'll find ten for whom these techniques are effective. Also, many people will have the "old you" stuck in their heads for a while. Even though they see and hear the new detached, relaxed, charming, and funny you, their brains interpret their experience of you as if you haven't changed. Give your old friends and family some time to see that the "new you" is for real, and not a fad.

7. Aren't I manipulating people by using these techniques?

All language choice is manipulation. If a realtor says the kitchen is cozy, is it small? It's probably both, but there's nothing wrong with putting the best spin on it. The skills in this book will help you meet the needs of people and give them what they want. Just because you know what they need and have methods to deliver the goods doesn't make you a manipulator. Using techniques to connect with others and bless them isn't manipulation.

8. I'm a gamer and pretty likeable. Why do you pick on gamers?

I have nothing against video games and play them some (I am always up for some zombie killing on Black Ops). However, my experience with games has been mostly negative. When I played them in my youth, they were escapes that allowed me to avoid contact with other humans in the real world. This may not be the case for you, but if you play all day, you may have to seriously evaluate why you're spending most of your life in a fantasy world instead of the real one. I can say this: if you're really, really into games, there's no way you're living up to your potential in the real world. Sorry, but it's true.

RECOMMENDED READING

FOR MORE INFORMATION AND STUDY

What follows are the resources that I've referenced throughout this book, either directly or indirectly. They have also greatly influenced me and given me concrete tips to increase my overall popularity and success.

Since you can always improve some aspect of your life, I'd highly recommend that you read a couple of these, especially if it's a topic where you are deficient (e.g. in reading body language). I've arranged them by category. Some of these books are more advanced, but mastering them could lead to more advanced results. This is a great chance to learn something valuable for less than the cost of a college class!

Body Language

Driver, Janine, and Mariska Van Aalst. You Say More Than You
    Think. New York: Crown, 2010.

Navarro, Joe, and Marvin Karlins. What Every Body Is Saying: An Ex-
    FBI Agent's Guide To Speed-Reading People. New York, NY:
    Collins Living, 2008.

Pease, Allan, and Barbara Pease. The Definitive Book Of Body
    Language. New York: Bantam, 2006.

Communication And Persuasion

Cialdini, Robert. Influence: Science And Practice. Boston: Pearson, 2009.

Garner, Alan. Conversationally Speaking. Los Angeles: Lowell House,
    1997.

O'Connor, Joseph, and John Seymour. Introducing NLP: Psychological
    Skills for Understanding and Influencing People. San Francisco,
    CA: Conari, 2011.

Rosenberg, Marshall. Nonviolent Communication: A Language Of Life:
    Create Your Life, Your Relationships, And Your World In
    Harmony With Your Values. Encinitas CA: Puddledancer Press,
    2008.

Confidence

Alexander, John. How To Become An Alpha Male. Raleigh, NC: Lulu, 2005.

McKenna, Paul, and Michael Neill. I Can Make You Confident: The Power To Go For Anything You Want! New York: Sterling, 2010.

Health, Fitness, and Good Looks

King, Ian, and Lou Schuler. The Book of Muscle: The World's Most Authoritative Guide To Building Your Body. Emmaus, PA: Rodale Books, 2003.

Roizen, Michael F., and Mehmet Oz. You, On A Diet: The Owner's Manual For Waist Management. New York: Free, 2009.

Roizen, Michael F., and Oz, Mehmet. You Staying Young: The Owner's Manual For Extending Your Warranty. New York: Free, 2007.

Making Money and Starting a Business

DeMarco, M. J. The Millionaire Fastlane: Crack The Code to Wealth and Live Rich For A Lifetime! Phoenix, AZ: Viperion, 2011.

Friedman, Nick, Omar Soliman, and Daylle Deanna Schwartz. Effortless Entrepreneur: Work Smart, Play Hard, Make Millions. New York: Three Rivers, 2010.

Mindfulness And Meditation

Davich, Victor. 8 Minute Meditation: Quiet Your Mind. Change Your Life. New York: Perigee Trade, 2004.

Kabat-Zinn, Jon. Mindfulness For Beginners: Reclaiming The Present Moment – And Your Life. Louisville, CO: Sounds True, 2011.

Success Principles

Bandler, Richard. Get The Life You Want: The Secrets To Quick And Lasting Change With Neuro-Linguistic Programming. Deerfield Beach, FL: Health Communications, 2008.

Bandler, Richard, and Garner Thomson. The Secrets to Being Happy. IM Press Inc., 2011.

Bennett, David, Jonathan Bennett, and Joshua Wagner. Say It Like You Mean It: How To Use Affirmations And Declarations To Create The Life You Want. Columbus, OH: Theta Storm Press, 2011.

Lieberman, David J. Get Anyone to Do Anything and Never Feel Powerless Again: Psychological Secrets to Predict, Control, and Influence Every Situation. New York: St. Martin's, 2000.

Works Cited

References

Chapter 1

1. http://www.listal.com/list/celebrities-were-bullied-school

Chapter 3

2. http://neuro.psychiatryonline.org/article.aspx?articleID=1213973

Chapter 13

3. http://www.mayoclinic.com/health/stress-relief/SR00034

4. http://www.psychologytoday.com/blog/the-possibility-paradigm/201106/are-you-meeting-your-laugh-quota-why-you-should-laugh-5-year-ol

5. https://www.msu.edu/~jdowell/monro.html

6. http://myweb.brooklyn.liu.edu/jlyttle/Humor/Theory.htm

Chapter 21

7. http://www.ew.com/ew/article/0,,313745,00.html

Chapter 22

8. http://www.celebritynetworth.com/richest-athletes/nfl/brian-bosworth-net-worth/

Chapter 26

9. http://well.blogs.nytimes.com/2011/03/23/whats-your-biggest-regret/

10. http://www.dailymail.co.uk/news/article-2106983/We-spend-45mins-week-dwelling-regrets--Electric-Zebra-survey.html

Chapter 30

11. http://www.dailymail.co.uk/news/article-2192748/Almost-famous-Student-hires-bodyguards-paparazzi-entourage-pranks-New-York-believing-world-famous-celebrity.html

Chapter 32

12. http://www.csun.edu/science/health/docs/tv&health.html

Chapter 34

13. http://www.dailymail.co.uk/femail/article-419040/Women-talk-times-men-says-study.html

thepopularman.com

Visit Our Website To:

Order Books

Download Videos and MP3s

Participate In Webinars

Sign Up For Consulting

Register For Events In Your Area

Join Our Mailing List

For More Great Life-Changing Resources:

Theta Hill

Thetahill.com

Theta Hill Press

Thetahillpress.com

The Popular Teen

Thepopularteen.com

Popular Teacher

Popularteacher.com

Made in the USA
San Bernardino, CA
11 October 2017